# UNITED STATES ARMY IN WORLD WAR II

# Reader's Guide

*Compiled and edited*

*by*

*Richard D. Adamczyk*
*Morris J. MacGregor*

MILITARY INSTRVCTION

*CENTER OF MILITARY HISTORY*
*UNITED STATES ARMY*
*WASHINGTON, D.C., 1992*

Library of Congress Catalog Card Number: 47–46404

Published volumes of the United States Army in World War II may be obtained through bookstores or by an order addressed to *Superintendent of Documents, Government Printing Office, Washington, D.C. 20402*, enclosing a check or money order for the price of the volumes.

CMH Pub 11–9

For sale by the U.S. Government Printing Office
Superintendent of Documents, Mail Stop: SSOP, Washington, DC 20402-9328
ISBN 0-16-037817-6

# Foreword

The United States Army in World War II series describes the organization, plans, and operations of the War Department and the Army, in the zone of interior and in all of the Army's five theaters of operations from 1939 to 1945. Since the Army authorized the project in 1946, seventy-eight volumes have been or are being published representing an organized treasury of knowledge on the world's greatest conflict. Behind them lies one of the largest masses of records and recollections ever produced. These documents, including those of the enemy, have been explored by professional historians, with the cooperation of a host of participants and with all the facilities and assistance that the Office of the Chief of Military History and its successor, the Center of Military History, could provide to ensure that this endeavor was as comprehensive, accurate, and objective as possible. The final result has provided commanders and staff officers, historians, and students—military and civilian alike—with an unprecedented professional guide to past experience as they seek light on the uncertain path ahead.

But the volumes are large and readers who need the knowledge contained in them are often pressed for time. Although each volume contains its own analytical index, a given subject may be discussed from various points of view in a number of volumes. The present pamphlet thus attempts to furnish the seeker of information with a finding aid which will enable him to profit more readily from the great investment of resources that the Army has devoted to extending his knowledge. This work supersedes *Reader's Guide II*, published in 1960. Criticisms and suggestions that look to the improvement of the present *Guide* will be welcomed.

Washington, D.C.                                         HAROLD W. NELSON
26 February 1992                                         Brigadier General, U.S. Army
                                                        Chief of Military History

# Preface

This pamphlet contains a brief analytical description of each volume in the United States Army in World War II series published to date or to be published in the near future. These sketches have, in most cases, been prepared by the author at the request of the Chief Historian in his capacity as General Editor of the series. Each synopsis is followed by a list of "key topics" found in the volume and in most cases their chapter location. In addition, a pamphlet index is included which refers to both the lists of key topics and the subject matter in the descriptive sketches. With its aid, the reader should be able to find information bearing on a specific topic that may be located in several volumes, which touch on different aspects of a problem or an event. However, neither the topic lists nor the pamphlet index are exhaustive, and should be supplemented by reference to the analytical index that is contained in each published volume.

The admonition which concluded the preface of *Reader's Guide I* bears repeating: "The descriptive sketches that appear in the following pages are not resumes or guts of the volumes. They do not provide pat answers but then neither does history. History is a vicarious story that cannot be experienced except through participation in the event or through reading. History's value lies in qualifying the reader to see events and problems as conditioned by their context and their sequence in time, not in isolation. Only extensive reading can give this qualification, which is the beginning of wisdom. It is hoped this pamphlet may help to get at the heart of the matter in which the reader is chiefly interested at any particular time."

Washington, D.C.                                               JEFFREY J. CLARKE
26 February 1992                                               Chief Historian
                                                               Center of Military History

# Contents

# The War Department

# The War Department

The eight volumes comprising The War Department subseries describe the achievements of the United States in becoming the Allied "arsenal of democracy" during the Second World War. These volumes also examine how the process of establishing and attaining truly astronomical war production objectives forever changed the structure of the United States economy. Highlighted are the myriad of problems associated with the allocation of limited resources and the organization and the processes involved in the execution of global war strategy. The volumes reveal the war as a transitional period for the nation, an era when the suspicions and fears of entangling alliances were replaced by an era of international cooperation and integration. This subseries thus traces the story of the hopes and fears, the triumphs and struggles of the Army confronting a world at war, and the monumental changes it undertook to meet that challenge.

**CHIEF OF STAFF: PREWAR PLANS AND PREPARATIONS**. By *Mark Skinner Watson*. (1950, 1985, 1991; 551 pages, 5 tables, 4 charts, 11 illustrations, bibliographical note, glossary, index, CMH Pub 1–1.)

From September 1938 to 7 December 1941 it became increasingly probable that the United States would have to fight in World War II. The central theme of this volume is the decisions and recommendations made by General Marshall as Chief of Staff with a view to preparing the Army for that event. The author explores and presents the successive situations and problems that confronted the Chief of Staff in making these decisions and recommendations, in order to enable the reader to see why and how historic judgments were reached and then to show how and through whom they were translated into action. Since General Marshall and the officers under him were involved in almost every problem confronting the nation in the decisive years covered, this book is a slice of national history.

In 1938–39 the Army was ill prepared even to defend the nation against attack; the public and Congress were determined to avoid war and ignorant of military requirements. The foreign policy of the United States was in debate, and the policies that the President followed in this period of doubt soon raised a conflict between the request for aid and the demands of national rearmament. Amid this confusion the services had to prepare for the worst. The present volume is an account of the methodical and often inspired planning and preparations, repeatedly interrupted and readjusted, but pursued until order emerged from confusion, so that, despite the shock of Pearl Harbor, the nation could within a year pass to the offensive in a two-front war.

Within the scope of the Army's own planning and preparations the book includes subjects that, for the period after Pearl Harbor, will be treated in many separate volumes of the United States Army in World War II—strategy, logistics, the mobilization and organization of men and industrial resources, recruiting and training of troops and officers, the role of air power, and the defense of the Western Hemisphere. The author considers these and other topics in their complex interrelationships during the instructive early period of uncertainty, overstrain, improvisation, trial and error, and radical readjustments. It is a necessary preface to the accounts of the war itself.

Key topics:

1. Military unpreparedness and its costs (Ch. II).
2. Rearmament under emergency conditions (Chs. V–VII, X, XI).
3. Recruitment and mobilization of the Army (Chs. VI, VII).
4. Program and problems of training (Ch. VII).
5. The aid-to-Allies policy versus the demands of rearmament (Ch. X).
6. The concept of a "balanced force" versus the President's policies and the rise of air power (Chs. IV, V, VI, IX).
7. Interrelations of foreign and military policy (Chs. IV, X, XII, XIII).
8. The role of the War Department General Staff in prewar strategic planning (Chs. I, IV, XII, XIII; see Index: "War Plans Division").
9. Early difficulties in coordinating military plans and industrial production (Chs. IV–VI, XI).
10. Progress toward a comprehensive supply plan: the Victory Program (Chs. X, XI).
11. Movement toward air autonomy within the Army (Chs. II, IV, IX; see also Index: "Army Air Forces").
12. The Chief of Staff and Congress (Chs. I, VI, VII; see Index: "Congress").
13. Coordination of U.S. and British plans and policies (Chs. IV, X, XII).
14. Prewar organization for the control of the Army, through the Chief of Staff, and its coordination, particularly with the Navy (Chs. I, III).
15. Evolution of the General Staff, 1921–41 (Ch. III).
16. The origins and adoption of lend-lease (Ch. X).
17. Preparations to defend the Western Hemisphere (Ch. XIV).
18. The decision to reinforce the Philippines (Ch. XIII).
19. The War Department's share in the responsibility for the surprise at Pearl Harbor (Ch. XV).
20. General Marshall and the principle of unity of (inter-Allied) command (Ch. XII).
21. Selection and promotion of officers (see Index: "Officers").

**WASHINGTON COMMAND POST: THE OPERATIONS DIVISION**. By *Ray S. Cline*. (1951, 1985, 1990; 413 pages, 4 charts, 4 illustrations, 2 appendixes, bibliographical note, glossaries, index, CMH Pub 1–2.)

This is the history of the agency through which General George C. Marshall exercised his paramount authority over the Army's activities, at home and overseas, from 9 March 1942 to the end of the war. From the Operations Division (OPD) he staffed his relations with the Navy and with other authorities, national and international. The Operations Division was also the source within the War Department on which General Marshall, both as the Army Chief of Staff and as a member of the Joint and Combined Chiefs of Staff, relied for advice and assistance in matters of strategy.

OPD, originally called War Plans Division (WPD), was a division of the General Staff, added to the "Gs" in 1921. The reorganization of the War Department in March 1942 pushed other divisions—G–1, G–3, and G–4—back into a position, then orthodox, that has been described as "thinking about military activities without participating in them." Moving at the same time in the opposite direction, that reorganization converted WPD into a central command post, with the operative functions of a field headquarters. OPD, a whole staff in itself, coordinated the other General Staff divisions, the three continental commands (Army Ground Forces, Army Air Forces, and Army Service Forces), and the Army commands overseas, including the great theaters of operations. OPD prepared General Marshall's orders to overseas commands and represented their views and needs to him. It became in effect his global command post. Through OPD he projected the strategic and operational views of the Army and its requirements in manpower and materiel across the whole field of wartime activities.

OPD was, in short, the organizational solution applied to the knottiest problem of high command, reconciling the requirements of administrative and operational decentralization with the necessity for effective supervision and unified control of worldwide operations. The present volume is an "institutional biography" of this agency, on which General Marshall relied heavily to give effect to his authority as supreme Army commander. Its origins, problems, conflicts, organization, personnel, development, and effectiveness and the methods and influence of its successive chiefs (Maj. Gen. Dwight D. Eisenhower, Lt. Gen. Thomas T. Handy, and Lt. Gen. John E. Hull) and their principal assistants can here be studied in detail.

The light this study throws on the relations of staff assistance and command gives it a special value for officers preparing for General Staff duty. The precedents it presents and the analogies it suggests make it invaluable as an aid in the recurrent search for effective organization at the center of national military authority.

Key topics:

1. Evolution of the mechanism of strategic planning (Army) before and during the war, with emphasis on staff systems and procedures (Chs. II, IX, X, XII, XVII). (For the substantive history of strategy in World War II, see the volumes on *Strategic Planning for Coalition Warfare*.)

2. The Army's concepts and influence in the development of American and Allied strategy (Chs. IX, XII, XVII).

3. The linkage of strategic planning with the effective direction of operations (Chs. XI, XV).

4. The coordination of the zone of interior and active theaters in a war fought overseas (Chs. IX, X, XIV).

5. The mechanics and operation of the joint staff committees before and during World War II (Chs. II, XIII–XIV).

6. Coordination of military planning and foreign policy in war (Chs. VI, XVI).

7. The role and functioning of the General Staff, War Department (Chs. I, II, VI).

8. Structure and functioning of the War Department, 1921–42 (Chs. I–VII).

9. Failure of staff work as a factor in the surprise at Pearl Harbor (Ch. V).

10. GHQ and WPD, 1940–42 (Chs. II, IV). (For a supplementary account, see "Origins of the Army Ground Forces: General Headquarters, United States Army, 1940–42," in *The Organization of Ground Combat Troops*, pp. 1–156.)

11. Wartime conferences of the Allies, with emphasis on staff preparations and procedures in debate: ARCADIA (Ch. V); Casablanca, TRIDENT, QUADRANT, and SEXTANT (Ch. XII).

12. BOLERO planning (Ch. IX).

13. Planning for SLEDGEHAMMER, ROUNDUP, HUSKY, OVERLORD, and ANVIL (see Index).

14. Planning for TORCH (Ch. X).

15. Planning for the final defeat of Japan, including the decision to use the atom bomb (Ch. XVII).

16. Comparison of OPD with organization of the Army General Staff under the National Security Act of 1947 (Ch. XVIII).

**STRATEGIC PLANNING FOR COALITION WARFARE: 1941–1942**. By *Maurice Matloff* and *Edwin M. Snell*. (1953, 1986, 1990; 454 pages, 3 charts, 12 illustrations, 7 appendixes, bibliographical note, glossaries, index, CMH Pub 1–3.)


Strategy means strategic concepts, plans for executing these concepts, and an application of national power designed to bring the enemy to terms. In World War II the production of strategic plans became a major industry in the military establishment. The main theme of this book is the history of that industry, as far as the War Department was concerned, to the end of 1942.

The basic strategic concepts of the Allies were embodied in the decisions reached in 1941 to treat Germany as the number one enemy and to wage unlimited war. This book is focused on the process by which these concepts were translated into strategic plans. It tells how national strategic plans were made, unmade, and remade. More particularly the authors are concerned with the Army's concepts of strategy and its efforts to get them accepted. Their book is therefore indispensable to military planners. But the treatment is so broadly conceived and so thorough that the book brings a wealth of information to bear on the whole picture of Allied strategy. It lights up, on the one hand, the evolution of strategic concepts. It includes the discussions of the Allies in the great conferences where the fate of the Army's plans and proposals was finally decided.

The volume follows, on the other hand, the search for forces, supplies, and ships with which to achieve the strategic objectives decided on as necessary and feasible. Using all the available information on its theme in American records, it is an organized account of what it meant (and may mean again), in terms of American thought and military potentials and the requirements of combined action, to prepare for, plan, and mount a global coalition war.

For the student of strategy this volume has a special value because it deals with a period of beginnings. It was a time of political indecision, extreme military anxiety, grave disappointments, meager resources, and "cut and try" in an incessant effort to keep strategic plans realistic. Army planners had to resolve continued differences between their views and those of the Navy, and American planners had to learn how to deal with the British, who in this period were urging plans which, although framed within agreements "in principle," were diametrically opposed to those of the Americans. Throughout the period American planners, groping for procedures that would be effective in dealing with these and their other problems, were acting without adequate precedents in American experience and without an organized record of such precedents as existed. The lessons they learned, as these developed from the circumstances of the time, are here set forth for the benefit of their successors.

Key topics:

1. The interplay of military, political, economic, and sentimental factors in determining what to do and when to do it (Chs. I, II, IV, VIII, XII, XVII).

2. Interaction of deployment and strategic concepts (Chs. VI, VII, XIV, XVI).

3. Coordination of strategic planning and immediate military demands (Chs. III, IX, X, XV, XVI).

4. The role of logistical feasibility (Ch. XVI; this subject is extensively treated in *Global Logistics and Strategy: 1940–1943*).

5. Planning against scarce resources (Chs. V, VII, IX, XVI).

6. Correlation of strategy with industrial potentials (Chs. III, XVI).

7. Problems of planning for a two-front global war (Chs. I, III, V, VII).

8. Encirclement and peripheral attrition versus concentration on a knockout blow (Chs. II, V, VII, VIII, XVII).

9. Differences between the strategic outlook of the Army and the Navy and their coordination (Chs. VII, X, XII, XIII).

10. Integration of air concepts and plans with those of the Army and Navy (Chs. II, VI, VII, XV, XVII).

11. Prewar evolution of the ORANGE and RAINBOW plans (Chs. I–IV).

12. Anglo-American staff conversations (ABC–1; ARCADIA) (Chs. III, V).

13. The Victory Program (Chs. III, VIII; more fully treated in *Chief of Staff: Prewar Plans and Preparations, Global Logistics and Strategy: 1940–1943*, and *The Army and Economic Mobilization*).

14. Evolution of the BOLERO concept and plan as an Army contribution to American strategy (Chs. VII–VIII; see also: *Washington Command Post: The Operations Division, Global Logistics and Strategy: 1940–1943*, and *Cross-Channel Attack*).

15. The effect of limited warfare in the Pacific on deployment for unlimited war (Chs. VII, IX–XII, XVI).

16. The presidential decision to invade North Africa (TORCH) and its effect on American deployment and strategic plans (Chs. XII–XIV).

17. The introduction of the President's unconditional surrender formula (Ch. XVII).

18. Anglo-American plans and Soviet expectations (Chs. VI, IX, X, XII, XV).

19. The strategic outlook of the United States on the eve of the Casablanca Conference, January 1943 (Ch. XVII).

**STRATEGIC PLANNING FOR COALITION WARFARE: 1943–1944**. By *Maurice Matloff*. (1959, 1970; 640 pages, 5 tables, 1 map, 26 illustrations, 5 appendixes, bibliographical note and guide to footnotes, glossaries, index, CMH Pub 1–4.)

In this volume Dr. Matloff, coauthor of the preceding volume, carries the subject forward from the conference at Casablanca (January 1943) through the second Allied conference at Quebec (September 1944), applying essentially the same methods and approach as in the earlier volume.

During these years General Marshall and his strategic planners had to grapple with the problems of the offensive phase of coalition warfare. The book is a carefully studied and thoroughly documented exposition of the American case for concentration, first against Germany, then against Japan.

While the author looks at the war through the eyes of the Washington high command, he looks at the whole war, in order to explain American thought and the measures that the American war leaders took. The reader will therefore find here a study of the positions of Great Britain, the USSR (Union of Soviet Socialist Republics), and China and of their leaders, Churchill, Stalin, and Chiang Kai-shek, as well as of Roosevelt and the American military chiefs, as they sought to resolve strategic and political problems.

Their proposals were tested in the debates at the great conferences of the coalition, and this volume contains a full account of five of the most important of these: Casablanca, TRIDENT (at Washington, May 1943), Quebec (August 1943), Cairo-Tehran (November–December 1943), and second Quebec. The period covered witnessed the triumph of the proposal for which the Americans most vigorously contended—a massive drive at the heart of Germany at the earliest possible date, finally set for early June 1944. In his exposition, the author gives ample space to the development of a strategy for the defeat of Japan, which was primarily an American responsibility. In accounting for the final adoption of the grand design of Allied strategy, he describes the increasing proficiency of the Americans in the art of military negotiation and diplomacy and the effect on strategy of the growing military weight of the United States and the USSR in the coalition.

As in the first volume, American planning is related at every step to its basis in American resources of industrial capacity and manpower, in the war aims of the government, and in public support of the war. The crisis of adjustment to recognition in the fall of 1942 of the approaching limitations of manpower available for conversion into fighting forces; the increasing investment in air power; and General Marshall's decision to limit American ground combat strength to ninety divisions are described in their relation to strategy. In these critical decisions on military policy, as well as in his role in decisions on strategy under debate with America's allies, General Marshall emerges as the principal American architect of military victory.

Key topics:

1. The interplay of military, economic, and political factors in strategic decisions (Introduction, Chs. I, VI, VII, X, XI, XVI, XXI).

2. Interaction of strategic concepts and the requirements of logistics and deployment (Chs. II, XI, XIV, XVI, XVII, XVIII, XX, XXIII). (For this and the following topic, see also both *Global Logistics and Strategy* volumes.)

3. The influence of problems of production and manpower on strategy (Introduction, Chs. V, VIII, XI, XVII, XVIII, XXIII).

4. Concentration on a knockout blow versus a strategy of encirclement and peripheral attrition (Introduction, Chs. I, II, III, VI, VIII, X, XI, XVI, XVIII, XX).

5. Divergences in strategic outlook of the Army and Navy and their coordination (Chs. II, IV, IX, XIV, XX, Epilogue).

6. Integration of air concepts and plans with those of the ground forces and Navy (Chs. I–IV, VI, IX, XIV).

7. Techniques of military diplomacy and negotiation (Chs. I, V, VI, X, XIII, XV, XVI, XXIII).

8. Relations between military planning and war aims (Introduction, Chs. I, XV, XVI, XVIII, XXII, XXIII, Epilogue).

9. President Roosevelt as Commander in Chief and war leader (Introduction, Chs. I, V, VI, X, XV, XVI, XXI, XXIII, Epilogue).

10. The major international conferences of midwar (Chs. I, VI, X, XIII, XVI, XXIII).

11. Problems of limited versus unlimited war (Introduction, Chs. XIV, XVII, XX, XXIII, Epilogue).

12. The effect on coalition strategy of changes in the balance of military power within the coalition (Chs. XVI, XXII, XXIII, Epilogue).

13. The unconditional surrender formula as a war aim (Chs. I, XVI, XVIII, XXIII, Epilogue).

14. The OVERLORD decision in its global framework (Chs. VIII, X–XIII, XV–XVI).

15. The decision to limit the U.S. ground army to ninety divisions (Chs. V, VIII, XVIII).

16. The Combined Bomber Offensive, the B–29, and the role of air power (Chs. I, III, IV, VI, IX, X, XIV, XIX, XXI, Epilogue).

17. Anglo-American plans and Soviet expectations (Introduction, Chs. I, XIII, XVI, XXII, Epilogue).

18. The China problem in politico-military strategy (Introduction, Chs. IV, VI, IX, X, XIV, XVI, XIX, XXI, Epilogue).

19. Paralleling Pacific with Mediterranean advances (Chs. IV, IX, XIV, XVI).

20. The decision for the southern France operation (Chs. XVI, XVIII, XXI).

21. The problem of neutrals: Spain and Turkey (Chs. I, II, XI, XVIII, XXII).

22. Expansion and distribution of American military power (Chs. XVII, XXIII, Apps. A, D, E).

**GLOBAL LOGISTICS AND STRATEGY: 1940–1943**. By *Richard M. Leighton* and *Robert W. Coakley*. (1955, 1984; 780 pages, 25 tables, 19 charts, 9 maps, 59 illustrations, 9 appendixes, bibliographical note, glossaries, index, CMH Pub 1–5.)

This volume covers U.S. Army logistics, primarily of ground forces, in its relation to global strategy during the period of American preparation for World War II and the first eighteen months of participation. It forms the capstone for the structure of histories dealing with logistical activities, of which such theater histories as *Logistical Support of the Armies* and *The Persian Corridor and Aid to Russia*, the War Department volumes on materiel procurement and industrial relations, and the technical service volumes provide the base. It is a companion piece to *Strategic Planning for Coalition Warfare: 1941–1942* and *Washington Command Post: The Operations Division*, since it treats logistics on the same general plane as that on which these volumes treat strategy.

The point of view is that of the central administration in Washington—Joint and Combined Chiefs of Staff, the War Department General Staff, and the Services of Supply. The dramatis personae are the officials of these agencies and of their civilian counterparts such as the War Shipping Administration and War Production Board; theater commanders; the U.S. President and British Prime Minister and their advisers; and other officials of the Allied governments. The major areas with which the volume deals are those that most concerned the high command—global aspects of transportation, division of resources among theaters, allocation of materiel to Allied nations, coordination of logistical support of joint Army-Navy operations, development of effective planning techniques for anticipating requirements in both men and materiel, organizational and administrative difficulties in mobilizing and expanding the nation's military power, the delicate relationships between strategy and logistics, and the frictions of interagency and inter-Allied coordination in these fields. The most persistent theme is the chronic, pervasive competition for resources—between theaters, between services, and between nations engaged in a coalition war.

The story of logistical plans and operations is developed concurrently with that of the evolution of the central administration that carried them on. This evolution of administration involved the wartime reshaping of Army organization, the creation of new joint and combined agencies, and the definition of relationships between civilian and military authority in such fields as shipping and war production.

The emphasis is on materiel rather than personnel, though troop shipping and service troops are treated in some detail, and the general problem of military manpower is outlined. Requirements for munitions and their allocation and distribution provide the central thread; industrial mobilization and war production are discussed only insofar as they affected these processes. In the prewar period the focus is on materiel shortages and competing needs of the expanding U.S. Army and those nations to whom American aid was pledged under the Lend-Lease Act. This theme continues into the post–Pearl Harbor period, but the emphasis shifts to the shortage of shipping—the primary factor in shaping all strategic and logistical plans during 1942 and early 1943. The volume describes how the American effort at first centered on strengthening positions in the Pacific, then shifted to preparations for early invasions of Europe, then to invasion of North Africa. Subsidiary efforts were devoted to supporting the British in the Middle East, developing supply routes to the USSR, and securing the Allied base in India for support to China. The result was a dispersion of resources that American strategic planners vainly resisted.

Specific logistical problems in each area growing out of this dispersion are treated in the "operational" chapters (VI, VII, XIV–XXI); concurrent development of policies, procedures, and organization for the long pull in Chapters VIII–XIII. A final section (XXII–XXVI) brings all of these developments into focus in the period of the Casablanca Conference (January 1943) and after. Considerable emphasis is devoted to the complexities of administering military lend-lease aid—the establishment of an Anglo-American common pool of supplies, the machinery for allocating materiel from it in accordance with strategic need, and the peculiar problems arising in the delivery of supplies to the USSR, China, the Middle East, and French North Africa (III, IV, X, XI, XVIII–XXI). A concluding chapter surveys the problems of logistical planning and salient features of the Army's logistical effort through spring 1943.

Key topics:

1. Historical development of the logistical function, evolution of the term logistics, and current conceptions of its meaning (Introductory).

2. Expansion and rearmament of the U.S. Army in 1940–41 and Army plans for global war (Chs. I–V).

3. Organization for logistics—U.S. Army, joint, and combined (Chs. IX, X, XIII, XXIV).

4. Relation of military requirements programs to strategy and to production capabilities (Chs. V, VIII, XI, XXII, XXIII, XXVII).

5. The system of pooling and allocating munitions among allies in a coalition war (Chs. X–XI, XVIII, XXI).

6. Emergence of the landing craft problem in 1942 and early 1943 (Chs. XIV–XVII, XXV).

7. Delivery of lend-lease military supplies to the USSR under the First and Second Soviet Protocols (Chs. IV, XX–XXI).

8. Specific logistical problems of operations in the British Isles, Australia, the Pacific islands, India, China, North Africa, and Iran in the perspective of global supply and shipping requirements (Chs. XIV–XXI).

9. Case studies in logistical plans and preparations—expeditions to the South Pacific and North Africa (TORCH) in 1942 (Chs. VII, XVI–XVII).

10. Impact of British import needs on the Allied military effort (Chs. XXV–XXVI).

11. Army supply procedures and policies, especially for overseas supply; the Army system for calculating requirements and distributing scarce items (Chs. XII, XIII, XXIII).

12. Army machinery for administering military lend-lease (Chs. III, X).

13. Service troop requirements (Chs. XIII–XXI).

14. Procedures and organization for joint Army-Navy logistical planning and operations (Chs. VII, XV, XXIV).

**GLOBAL LOGISTICS AND STRATEGY: 1943–1945.** By *Robert W. Coakley* and *Richard M. Leighton.* (1968, 1989; 889 pages, 34 tables, 5 charts, 8 maps, 49 illustrations, 8 appendixes, bibliographical note, glossaries, index, CMH Pub 1–6.)

Like its predecessor, *Global Logistics and Strategy: 1940–1943*, this volume treats U.S. Army logistics from the point of view of the high command and staffs in Washington; it continues the preceding volume's narrative from the spring of 1943, on the eve of the TRIDENT Conference in May, to the surrender of Japan. Space limitations have precluded coverage of the logistical issues involved in repatriation, occupation, and disposal of surplus property in the immediate aftermath of the war. Together the two volumes form the capstone of the logistical histories, of which the War Department volumes on economic mobilization, industrial relations, and aircraft procurement; such theater histories as *Logistical Support of the Armies* (European theater) and *The Persian Corridor and Aid to Russia*; and the technical service volumes provide the base. Viewing logistics and strategy as parallel and interacting activities, this volume treats logistics on the same plane as the War Department volumes on strategic planning and operational direction treat strategy—for example, from the point of view of the central administration in Washington. The immense cast of characters, not limited to faceless agencies such as the Joint and Combined Chiefs of Staff, the War Shipping Administration, the War Department General Staff, and OPD (Operations Division of the General Staff), includes such legendary figures as President Roosevelt; British Prime Minister Churchill; "Gissimo" Chiang Kai-shek; Generals Marshall, MacArthur, and Stilwell; Admiral King; and, of course, the Army Service Forces' Commanding General, Lt. Gen. Brehon B. Somervell, and his chief subordinate, Maj. Gen. Leroy Lutes.

The book focuses on the myriad problems involved during the last two years of World War II in the division of resources among nations and theaters in a global conflict and on the logistical organization and processes involved in the formation and execution of strategy. This broad approach results in the same omissions that characterized the 1940–43 volume: the book does not cover detailed logistical operations at lower levels; it does not treat internal logistics in overseas theaters except as necessary to establish the context for decisions at the center; and it is primarily concerned with ground force logistics, viewed in its interactions with air (especially strategic air) and naval logistics. The omitted subject areas have been adequately covered in other volumes of the U.S. Army in World War II and in various publications sponsored by the Offices of Air Force History and of Naval History— upon which the present authors have drawn heavily in preparing this volume.

Unlike the 1940–43 volume, this work employs a topical approach to the extent of treating supply organization and procedures (Part 2) and lend-lease and civilian supply (Part 7) in groups of chapters separate from the mostly chronological, "operational" narratives tracing strategic-logistical planning for the great offensive campaigns of the Western Allies during 1943–45. These operational chapters also treat the war against the European Axis (Parts 1, 3, 4) and the war against Japan (Parts 5, 6) in separate compartments, while still making clear the essential interconnections between the two. A final chapter (XXXII) analyzes, in broad strokes, the evolving relationship between logistics and strategy over the entire span of the war.

Among the distinctive and valuable contributions of these two volumes to the Army's official World War II history, special mention should be given the examination in depth of four major spheres of wartime logistics: foreign aid, assault and cargo shipping, and logistical organization and method. Foreign aid is mainly the story of lend-lease, the system of pooling and allocating munitions among coalition allies, primarily to the British Empire and the Soviet Union (XXV–XXIX); it also includes civilian supply (XXX, XXXI): the responsibility assumed by the Army, from mid-1943 on, for provision of essential services and material needs of civilian populations in liberated and occupied territories. Assault shipping (landing ships and craft and amphibian vehicles) was an indispensable prerequisite, hardly foreseen before the war and tardily and grudgingly recognized after it began, for the numerous over-the-beach landings on hostile shores that spearheaded many offensives in the Atlantic, Mediterranean, Pacific, and Far East theaters. The emergence of the problem is treated in the 1940–43 volume; this book describes the "crash" production programs of 1943 and 1944 and the severe limitations that shortages of this critical resource imposed on the scope and range of virtually every amphibious operation from mid-1943 on. Cargo shipping was the basic instrument for carriage of war materiel across seas and oceans, and thus a key element in the coordination of operations in a multitheater conflict. In a war of many bottlenecks, assault shipping and cargo shipping were the most persistent and salient. Organization and method, probably the most esoteric aspects of logistics, are nevertheless its inescapable essence in what Jomini called a "science of detail" and of course required reading for future planners of big wars.

Building on the solid foundation laid in the predecessor volume, this study devotes three chapters (IV, V, VI) to an exposition of the mature wartime system of 1943–45—organization, requirements/production, and wholesale distribution—including the mysteries of the joint (such as Army-Navy) logistical system and its interaction with the largely civilian machinery for management of the war economy. Three more chapters and parts of another (XVI–XVIII, XX, XXIV) describe the complex variations of the system developed to support the war of vast oceanic distances and primitive infrastructure in the Pacific, including redeployment for the single-front war in 1945. In addition, the evolution of organization and method is a major theme of the foreign aid story in Chapters XXV–XXXI.

Key topics:

1. An overview of logistics in World War II—major trends and developments (Ch. XXXII).

2. Strategic-logistical planning and buildup for the cross-Channel invasion, 1943–44 (Chs. I–III, VII–XV).

3. Strategic-logistical planning for the invasion of Sicily (Chs. II–III).

4. Strategic-logistical planning for Allied operations in the Mediterranean, 1943–45 (Chs. VII–IX, XI, XIII–XV).

5. Strategic-logistical planning for operations in the China-Burma-India Theater (Ch. XXI).

6. Organization and processes for logistical planning: U.S. Army, joint, and combined (Chs. IV–VI).

7. The role of logistics in strategic planning (Ch. XXXII).

8. The relation of military requirements to strategy and production capabilities (Chs. V, VI, XXIII).

9. The system of pooling and allocating munitions among coalition allies (Chs. XXV–XXIX).

10. The role of ocean shipping in global war (Chs. II, III, X, XII, XIV, XV, XIX, XXII, XXIII).

11. Assault shipping in Allied strategy in World War II (Chs. I–III, VII–XV, XVII, XX, XXXII).

12. Assault shipping at the midwar Allied conferences in 1943 (Chs. III, VIII, XI).

13. Military lend-lease to the USSR in the later war years (Ch. XXVII).

14. Military lend-lease to liberated nations in World War II (Ch. XXVIII).

15. Military lend-lease to Latin America in World War II (Ch. XXVIII).

16. Military lend-lease to China, 1943–45 (Ch. XXIX).

17. The Army and civilian supply (Chs. XXX–XXXI).

18. Joint logistics in the war against Japan, 1943–44 (Chs. XVI–XIX).

19. Army logistics in the Pacific, 1943–44 (Ch. XX).

20. Logistics of the one-front war, 1945 (Ch. XXIV).

**THE ARMY AND ECONOMIC MOBILIZATION.** By *R. Elberton Smith.* (1959, 1985; 749 pages, 63 tables, 4 charts, 11 illustrations, bibliographical note, glossaries, index, CMH Pub 1–7.)

No ingredient of the power with which the Allies inflicted defeat on their enemies in World War II is less in dispute than the overwhelming superiority in the materiel of war that they ultimately developed. Equally evident is the fact that the United States took the lead in producing the great variety and huge quantities of munitions, military equipment, supplies, and services that gave them this superiority. The present volume is a description and analysis of the basic problems, policies, and procedures with which the War Department, in cooperation with almost every other agency of government, was concerned in carrying out a nationwide program of economic mobilization.

This work traces the foundations of the achievement in the nation's experience of World War I and the planning for economic mobilization with which the War Department was charged in the period between the two wars. It describes, for each of the major substantive areas of economic mobilization, the nation's transition from a peacetime status through the eighteen-month "defense period" to the achievement of a full-fledged war economy.

Before production for war had reached its peak, planning for a return to a peacetime economy began, and the book in its concluding chapters describes this and the operations by which the vast machine was dismantled and reconverted. An "epilogue" chapter reviews and summarizes the effort of economic mobilization as a whole and presents the author's conclusions.

The volume concentrates on the basic issues as they appeared at the highest policy-making levels of the War Department—the Office of the Under Secretary of

War and the staff divisions of the Headquarters of the Army Service Forces. Nevertheless, in order to show the operational effects of the policies adopted, and in turn the reciprocal effects of operations on policy, the study includes many of the activities of the Army's actual procuring arms and services.

These operations are set forth in detail in the volumes of the United States Army in World War II devoted to each of the technical services. The present volume, in addition to forming the capstone of these as far as they relate to economic mobilization and reconversion, is closely related to such others in the series as both *Global Logistics and Strategy* volumes, *The Army and Industrial Manpower,* and *The Organization and Role of the Army Service Forces.* It may also be read to advantage in conjunction with the various histories, official and unofficial, that describe the wartime activities of other governmental agencies on the home front.

Key topics:

1. The following subject areas are discussed throughout:

a. Economics of war.

b. Relation between economic, political, and other factors in the development and administration of economic control systems.

c. Production feasibility of wartime requirement programs.

d. Organization and administration of military procurement; military versus civilian responsibility for procurement; quantities, varieties, and special characteristics of military procurement items.

e. Contract placement problems: selection of contractors, development and use of the negotiated contract, preliminary contractual instruments, and contract forms.

f. Wartime pricing problems: effects of the decline of competition in wartime; pricing policy as a means of economizing real resources; dilemmas posed by the requirement of "close pricing"; effects of ceiling prices upon military procurement; and alternative and complementary solutions to wartime pricing problems.

2. Problems of small business in the placement and administration of war contracts (Ch. XVIII).

3. Financing of military and industrial facilities (Chs. XIX–XXI).

4. War Department procurement planning—1920–40 (Ch. III).

5. Nationwide industrial mobilization planning—1920–40 (Ch. IV).

6. Methods of determining military requirements (Chs. VI–VIII).

7. Nature and administration of Army cost-plus-a-fixed-fee contracts in World War II (Ch. XII).

8. Pricing in fixed-price contracts; origin and development of progressive pricing articles (Ch. XIII).

9. Contract renegotiation—origin and nature, principles, policies, and results in World War II (Chs. XV–XVI).

10. Nature and administration of "tax amortization" provisions for rapid write-off of capital facilities in World War II (Ch. XX).

11. Evolution and administration of the priorities system in World War II (Chs. XXIII–XXIV).

12. Origin, adoption, and administration of the Controlled Materials Plan (Ch. XXV).

13. Contract termination and settlement: basic policies, procedures, and results for World War II (Chs. XXVII–XXIX).

**THE ARMY AND INDUSTRIAL MANPOWER.** By *Byron Fairchild* and *Jonathan Grossman.* (1959, 1970; 291 pages, 3 tables, 2 charts, bibliographical note, glossary, index, CMH Pub 1–8.)

The administration and management of industrial labor, except in the Army's arsenals, were until World War I fields remote from the traditional responsibilities of the Army. In World War II the War Department found itself drawn into these areas to an unprecedented extent, not only by its concern for the output of munitions, but also by its new responsibilities regarding industry in such fields as the maintenance of security in war plants, the enforcement of labor laws and policies, and the administration of facilities forcibly seized by the government to avert stoppage of production by labor-management disputes. The present volume is not intended to be a comprehensive treatise; the aim, instead, is to illustrate by discussion of selected topics the nature of the problems the War Department faced in relation to the employment of industrial manpower and the policies and procedures that it developed to deal with them. This discussion is complementary to two other volumes on the subject of procurement, economic mobilization, and supply—*The Army and Economic Mobilization* and *Buying Aircraft: Materiel Procurement for the Army Air Forces*—as well as to the histories of the technical services.

Given the experience of World War I, the concern of the War Department with labor problems as an aspect of its broad responsibilities for procurement was recognized and was the subject of planning in the years between the two world wars. The labor planning and the organizational developments that occurred during World War II are described in Chapters I and II, which provide the background for the rest of the volume. Chapters III through V constitute a discussion of the restrictive factors affecting the use of the civilian labor force that either were anticipated or assumed important during the war. The authors next consider the problem of labor supply, which gained momentum toward the end of 1943, and the efforts of the Army to meet it (Chs. VI through IX). They describe the measures taken to recruit additional workers and the successful special project technique that was developed to deal with labor problems. The subject of Chapter X is the role of the Army as an instrument for enforcing the labor policies of the government. The use of Selective Service and the seizure of industrial facilities by the government as measures of enforcement are described. The volume concludes with a discussion of the attempts to obtain the enactment by Congress of some form of national service legislation (Ch. XI) and with a brief chronological survey (Ch. XII).

Key topics:

1. Labor clauses in procurement contracts.
2. Public opinion and the mobilization of labor.
3. Labor supply factors in contract placements and cutbacks.

4. The problem of minority groups in war industry.
5. The employment of foreign workers and prisoners of war.
6. The use of soldiers in war industry.
7. Compulsory service in war industry versus voluntary labor.
8. The relation between the strength of the Army and the size of the civilian labor force.

# The Army Ground Forces

# The Army Ground Forces

The War Department and the Army underwent a radical reorganization three months after the United States entered World War II. That reorganization consolidated the undeployed forces of the Army in the continental United States under three major commands—the Army Ground Forces (AGF), the Army Air Forces, and the Services of Supply (later the Army Service Forces). It also vested in the commanders of the first two of these great commands the responsibilities which had formerly been exercised by the chiefs of the arms and made these commanders responsible for the organization and training of the combat forces of the Army. These volumes, written during and immediately after the war by historians in the Headquarters, AGF, discuss the exercise of those responsibilities by that headquarters insofar as they pertained to the size and organization of the ground combat forces.

**THE ORGANIZATION OF GROUND COMBAT TROOPS.** By *Kent Roberts Greenfield, Robert R. Palmer*, and *Bell I. Wiley*. (1947, 1983; 540 pages, 24 tables, 11 charts, 5 illustrations, bibliographical note, glossaries, index, CMH Pub 2–1.)

This work opens with a history of General Headquarters (GHQ), U.S. Army, established in July 1940 under the direction of Lt. Gen. Lesley J. McNair, who would later command the Army Ground Forces. During the period of initial mobilization General Headquarters had the responsibility for training field forces, a task that in March 1942 was given to the Army Ground Forces. The history of GHQ is therefore essential to an understanding of the reorganization that brought the Army Ground Forces into existence. The remainder, and greater part, of the volume is a series of six studies focusing on major problems presented by the mobilization and organization of the ground combat army and the efforts of General McNair to solve them. A final study deals with the reorganization of the ground forces for redeployment against Japan.

The unpleasant discovery late in 1942 that the dual role of combatant power and "arsenal of democracy" was overtaxing the effective resources of the United States, in both manpower and industrial capacity, together with a continued shortage of shipping, forced the government to reconsider the size and shape of its military forces. As a consequence the ground forces underwent a drastic reorganization to meet limitations imposed by higher authority. General McNair welcomed this as an opportunity to produce leaner and more mobile organizations within the Army Ground Forces without loss of firepower and with a gain, as he believed, in capacity for offensive action. In general, he sought economy of force by combating the swing toward specialization that had occurred as the traditional arms were mechanized and motorized and as new arms sprang up around the development of instruments of war such as the tank and tank destroyer and antiaircraft artillery. He sought by a diversity of means for a better balance between specialized and general purpose units. He contended also for a better balance between combat and service forces. The two principles on which he counted most heavily were pooling and reinforcement. Since economy of forces continues to be jeopardized by the tendency toward specialization and overweight in noncombat elements, the successes and limitations of General McNair's drastic experiment in 1943, here presented and analyzed with reference to the conditions of World War II, should be instructive to those responsible for the effectiveness of the Army.

For the student of national policy the studies in this volume, particularly the studies of mobilization, have an instructive bearing on the question of how large an effective force the United States can deploy in a war fought overseas.

(In the lists that follow, the six studies comprised in this volume are arbitrarily assigned numerical designations 1 to 6.)

Key topics:

1. Training of field combat units in the period of emergency, 1941–42 (Study 1, Ch. II).

2. Origins of antitank and tank destroyer doctrine (Study 1, Ch. IV).

3. Early plans for the organization and use of armor (Study 1, Ch. III) and subsequent modifications (Study 4, Ch. V; Study 5, Chs. I and III, pp. 430ff.; Study 6, Ch. II).

4. Early problems of air-ground doctrine, coordination, and training (Study 1, Ch. VII).

5. Strength and distribution of ground forces in the Army, December 1941–April 1945, with analysis, comments, and conclusions (Study 2 and table).

6. The troop basis of the Army in World War II (Studies 2 and 6).

7. Mobilization: problems and history in World War II (Study 3).

8. Mobilization: effect of changes in war plans (Study 3, Ch. II).

9. Deceleration of the rate of mobilization to meet limitations of manpower, productive capacity, and shipping (Study 3, Ch. III).

10. Impact on the troop basis of events in theaters of operations (Study 3, Ch. IV).

11. Mobilization and deployment in first and second world wars compared (Study 3, Charts 1 and 2).

12. Tactical organization of the Army before and after 8 March 1942 (Study 4; Study 6, Ch. II).

13. Application of "streamlining" and the principles of pooling, flexible control, and reinforcement to the tactical organization of the Army in 1943 (Study 4, Chs. III–V, VII; Study 5, Ch. I) and the reaction in 1945 (Study 6).

14. Integration of new arms, armor, tank destroyers, antiaircraft artillery, and airborne forces into the ground army (Study 1, Chs. III, IV, VI; Study 4, Chs. III, V, VI; Study 5).

15. Reorganization for redeployment (Study 6).

16. Test and collapse in 1942 of the "GHQ concept" as developed between 1921

and 1940 (Study 1, Chs. I, IX, X).

17. GHQ as a command post for the control of overseas commands (Study 1, Chs. I, IX, and X; for transfer of this function to OPD, see *Washington Command Post: The Operations Division*, Chs. II, IV, VI, VII).

18. The Army's role in amphibious training, 1940–42 (Study 1, Ch. V).

19. Organization for defense of the continental United States (Study 1, Ch. VIII).

20. Authorized and actual enlisted strength of troop units (Study 3).

21. The heavy artillery program, 1942–44 (Study 3, Chart 6, and Index: "Heavy artillery").

22. The decision in favor of general purpose versus highly specialized large units (Study 4, Chs. V–VI).

23. Abandonment of the "Type" army and corps and the extension of the task force principle (Study 4, Ch. VII).

24. The struggle of AGF against overhead regarded as excessive (see Index: "Overhead").

25. Experiment with light divisions (Study 3, Ch. VI).

26. Abandonment of specialized divisions: cavalry, motorized, mountain, and jungle (Study 3, Ch. VI).

27. Organization of new arms for training (Study 5, Ch. II).

28. Typical redeployment experience of a division (Study 6, Ch. IV).

29. Effect of the point system (individual demobilization) on redeployment (Study 6, Ch. I).

30. Discussion of the total size of the ground combat force that the United States could deploy overseas (Study 3).

31. The adverse effects of mechanization and motorization on the transportability of ground forces and their mobility in the field (Study 4, Chs. II, V, and VI).

32. Initial organization and training of airborne units (Study 1, Ch. VI) and changes of organization in 1943 (Study 4, Ch. VI).

33. Conflicts between a balanced force structure and the demands of the combat arms, old and new (Study 5, Ch. I).

34. Headquarters organization, including the problem of size (see Index: "Headquarters").

**THE PROCUREMENT AND TRAINING OF GROUND COMBAT TROOPS.** By *Robert R. Palmer, Bell I. Wiley*, and *William R. Keast*. (1948, 1975, 1991; 696 pages, 36 tables, 4 charts, bibliographical note, glossaries, index, CMH Pub 2–2.)

The ten studies in this volume (in further references below arbitrarily assigned numerical designations 1 to 10) continue the series published in *The Organization of Ground Combat Troops*. Except for Studies 4 and 5, which deal with individual training in the service schools of the ground forces, they focus, like those in the previous volume, on major problems of the Army Ground Forces, the solutions applied to them by that command, and the success or failure of those solutions, considered in the context of events and policies of the time.

Studies 4 and 5 describe the wartime methods and operations of the military school system. One of the most persistent problems, one that affected all the others, was that of procuring quality personnel that could be transformed into combat troops capable of meeting effectively the complex requirements of World War II. As measured by the Army's general classification tests, the men allocated to the Army Ground Forces were inferior intellectually and physically to those allocated to the Army Air and Service Forces, as well as to those recruited by the Marine Corps and the Navy. Efforts to solve this problem, never fully successful, involved specialized training programs and constitute a subject of continuing concern.

Warned by the experience of World War I, the War Department adopted in 1940 the policy of fully preparing its combat organizations for battle before shipping them overseas. General McNair, both as chief of staff of GHQ from 1940 to 1942 and as Commanding General of the Army Ground Forces, made the training of large forces the principal goal of his efforts. The program of training he devised to this end, from small-unit training to the maneuvers of corps and armies, and the difficulties and disappointments he encountered in applying the program, receive close attention. The adverse effect of his policy on the training of the smaller nondivisional units of the ground forces is described in Study 8. General McNair also inherited, with the authority of the chiefs of arms vested in him in March 1942, responsibility for the procurement and training of replacements and the conduct of the individual training of officers and men in the service schools and officer candidate schools of the ground combat arms.

The replacement system broke down as it had in World War I. The consequent crises in the procurement and training of replacements are described in Studies 3 and 6. The changes that the Army Ground Forces, acting through its Replacement and School Command, introduced into the service schools in the interest of economy or efficiency are included in the description of those schools in Study 4. Study 10, on redeployment training, describes changes proposed in the light of 1942–45 experience as well as those required by immediate problems.

Key topics (*Org* is used in the lists below to refer to this work's companion volume *The Organization of Ground Combat Troops*):

1. Policies and problems of officer procurement (Study 2; see also *Org*, Study 1, Ch. II).

2. Training of ground units for combat (Studies 7, 8, 9; see also *Org*, Index: "Training").

3. Wartime training in the service schools of the ground arms (Studies 4 and 5).

4. The building and training of infantry divisions, interferences with training, and the effect of these (Study 7).

5. The training of nondivisional units in the Army Ground Forces: organization and programs (Study 8).

6. The replacement system in World War II (Study 3; see also Study 6 and Study 7, Ch. IV).

7. Replacement training (Study 6).

8. Effect of uncalculated demands on programs of training (Study 3, Ch. II; Study 6, Ch. IV; Study 7, Ch. IV and Tables 2 and 4; Study 8, Ch. III; Study 9, Ch. III; Study 10, Ch. II).

9. Impact of unexpected, or concentrated, losses on the provision and training of replacements (Study 3, Ch. II).

10. The Army classification system: its adverse effect on the ground arms (Study 1, Ch. I).

11. Effect of preferential assignment to the Army Air Forces on the personnel of the Army Ground Forces (Study 1, Ch. II).

12. The Army Specialist Training Program versus the demand for higher grade combat troops (Study 1, Ch. II).

13. Use of limited-service men in AGF units (Study 1, Ch. II).

14. The origins and effect of the Physical Profile System (Study 1, Ch. III).

15. Organization, training, and testing in the service schools (Study 4, Chs. II and III).

16. Methods used to ensure readiness of units for deployment overseas (Study 9).

17. Testing the effects of training (see Index: "Tests"; also *Org*, Study 1, Ch. II, and Index: "Tests").

18. Effects of the policy of individual (versus unit) battle replacements (Study 3, Ch. III).

19. Officer candidate schools (Study 5).

20. Organization and methods of the replacement training centers of the Army Ground Forces (Study 6).

21. Adjustments of replacement training to theater requirements (Study 6, Ch. IV).

22. The stripping of divisions for replacements and its effect on their battle readiness (Study 7, Ch. IV, and Tables).

23. Shortages of equipment and their effect on training (Study 7, Chs. II and III).

24. Organization of new arms for training (see *Org*, Study 5, Ch. II).

25. Use of maneuvers as a training device (Study 1, Ch. II).

# The Army Service Forces

# The Army Service Forces

This subseries describes and analyzes the military management of a vast complex of activities which during World War II fell generally into the field of logistics. In March 1942, in order to free General Marshall and the General Staff of a mass of administrative burdens, operational responsibility for the continental United States was delegated to three major commands: the Army Ground Forces (Lt. Gen. Lesley J. McNair), the Army Air Forces (Lt. Gen. Henry H. Arnold), and the Army Service Forces—at first the Services of Supply (Lt. Gen. Brehon B. Somervell). The present volume is a study of the third of these great commands, written by an author trained in political science and public administration, who was an adviser to General Somervell.

**THE ORGANIZATION AND ROLE OF THE ARMY SERVICE FORCES.** By *John D. Millett*. (1954, 1985; 494 pages, 3 tables, 7 charts, 8 illustrations, 9 appendixes, bibliographical note, glossary, index, CMH Pub 3–1.)

This work examines World War II from the viewpoint of the Commanding General of the Army Service Forces, Lt. Gen. Brehon B. Somervell. It is concerned with problems of materiel rather than manpower. A study in the problems of management, it deliberately dwells on the conflicts which arose inside and outside the command.

As a result of the 1942 reorganization General Somervell became the commander of the supply ("technical") and administrative services and of the nine corps areas of the United States. He also became the principal adviser to the Under Secretary of War and the Chief of Staff on logistical matters and was on occasion sent by them as a troubleshooter to theaters of operations. Inside the War Department General Somervell's interpretation of the necessary role of his organization brought it into conflict with the powerful Operations Division of the General Staff (OPD), particularly with regard to the relationship of strategy and supply (which are explored in Chapters IV and V) and also with regard to the jurisdiction of the Army Service Forces over the strongly entrenched chiefs of the supply and administrative services.

Outside the War Department the Commanding General, Army Service Forces, clashed with the War Production Board. The story of this conflict has been told elsewhere from the point of view of the War Production Board (in *The United States at War* [Washington, 1946], a publication of the Bureau of the Budget; and in

Donald M. Nelson, *Arsenal of Democracy* [New York, 1946]). In the present volume the position of the Army Service Forces is fully set forth (Chs. XIII–XV), the lessons derived from this conflict are discussed (Ch. XIX), and there is a recital of the less troubled relationships of the Army Service Forces with other civilian agencies (Chs. XVI–XVII) and with the Navy (Ch. XVIII).

General Somervell's capacity as a manager was challenged not only by the vastness of his command but even more by the diversity of tasks and agencies for which it was responsible. The work gives extended attention to the ASF chief's efforts to achieve an effective organization, particularly to his efforts to coordinate the technical services (Ch. XX), establish a unified field organization for service activities (Ch. XXI), rationalize his huge headquarters (Ch. XXII), and introduce into his command continuous improvements in management (Chs. XXIII, XXIV).

This volume presents the most instructive experiment made by the Army before 1954 in centralizing the command of logistical operations. To complete a study of the activities of the Army Service Forces, the reader should consult other volumes in the United States Army in World War II, such as both *Global Logistics and Strategy* volumes, *The Army and Economic Mobilization, The Army and Industrial Man-power,* and *Buying Aircraft: Materiel Procurement for the Army Air Forces; Washington Command Post: The Operations Division,* Chs. XIII–XIV; *The Persian Corridor and Aid to Russia,* Chs. X–XII; and the volumes in the technical service subseries, in which the Army Service Forces is observed from the point of view of its subordinate commands.

Key topics:

1. Wartime organization of the continental United States (the zone of interior) in a war fought overseas (Chs. I, II, IX, XX, XXI, XXIV).

2. Centralization versus decentralization in the wartime administration of supply in the zone of interior (Chs. XI, XX, XXI).

3. Coordination of the distribution of supplies between the zone of interior and theaters of operations (Chs. III–V, VII).

4. The problem of command relations in supplying combat forces in the zone of interior (Chs. VIII, XI).

5. Common versus separate supply for ground, air, and sea forces (Chs. VIII, XI, XVIII).

6. Relationships and conflicts of interest between military and civilian authority in the control of procurement and industrial mobilization for war (Chs. XIII–XVII, XIX).

7. The relation of strategy and logistics in military planning (Chs. III, VII).

8. Use of a "control" agency as a managerial device in a large military organization (Ch. XXIII).

9. Civilian versus military control of the wartime economy of the United States (Ch. XIX).

10. Administration of military lend-lease supplies (Chs. III, XVII). (For a fuller treatment, see both *Global Logistics and Strategy* volumes.)

11. The supply aspects of the reorganization of the War Department in March 1942 (Ch. II).

12. A case study of the problem of planning versus operational activity in defining the proper authority and functions of the General Staff (Chs. I, II, VII, X, XII).

13. The problem of controlling the size of military headquarters, for which a solution was not found in World War II (Ch. XXII).

# The Western Hemisphere

# The Western Hemisphere

The aggressive wartime strategy of the United States, concerted with its European Allies, into which it launched so promptly and with such a massive deployment of force after 7 December 1941, obscures the fact that its declared military policy before that date was defensive. In November 1938 President Roosevelt enunciated the doctrine that defense of the continental United States required, as the military objective of the nation, defense of the Western Hemisphere. This fixed the official goal for the efforts of the War Department until Pearl Harbor, and, in the view of the authors of these volumes, dominated its plans and preparations during the two years preceding the Destroyer-Base Agreement of September 1940. Even after that the requirements of hemisphere defense defined the framework within which the Army and its Air Forces put into effect the limited preparations and actions that were directed against the aggressions of Nazi Germany and Japanese imperialism. The area covered in these two volumes is vast and so are the topics.

**THE FRAMEWORK OF HEMISPHERE DEFENSE.** By *Stetson Conn* and *Byron Fairchild*. (1960, 1989; 470 pages, 1 map, bibliographical note, glossaries, index, CMH Pub 4–1.)

The new military policy of hemisphere defense enunciated in 1938 was a reaction to the increasing offensive potentiality of military aircraft. The continental United States could not at that time be invaded or seriously threatened unless the attack was backed by land-based air power. Hostile airplanes in significant numbers could not then be projected across the oceans, but they could be launched from bases established in other parts of the Western Hemisphere within striking distance of the United States and its possessions. The basic mission of the armed forces under the hemisphere defense policy was therefore to prevent the establishment of hostile air bases in the Western Hemisphere. Since eastern Brazil seemed to offer the most likely initial location for such bases, it became the focus of Army plans and actions for hemisphere defense.

In the early summer of 1940 the quick defeat of France and seemingly precarious position of Great Britain created an emergency that required much closer military ties between the United States and the other New World nations. Military collaboration with Canada evolved thereafter with a minimum of friction into a close partnership. Since the Latin American nations at that time had almost no military strength by modern standards, the United States had to assume almost complete responsibility for defending them against external attack. At the same time it had to avoid any infringement—real or imagined—on Latin American sovereignty. Aided by the trust inspired by the "Good Neighbor" policy of preceding years, the United States persuaded most of these nations to accept its pledges of armed support, and from June 1940 onward it entered into military collaboration with them to an unprecedented degree. This collaboration included a military association with Mexico almost as close as that with Canada—in marked contrast with the hostile attitude of Mexico toward the United States during World War I. The groundwork of successful collaboration with the other New World nations allowed the United States Army to begin to deploy its offensive strength overseas almost immediately after the Japanese attack.

The opening chapters of the present volume (I–VII) are an introduction to this story and to a sequel volume, *Guarding the United States and Its Outposts*. These chapters trace the evolution of the policy of hemisphere defense in the three years before Pearl Harbor, the gradual merging of hemisphere defense into the broader national policy of opposing German and Japanese aggression by all-out aid to peoples fighting the Axis, and the quick transition to offensive plans and preparations in December 1941. They describe the crises that faced or appeared to face the United States in May 1940 and again in May 1941 (Chs. II, V), the nature of the German and Japanese threats to the Western Hemisphere (Ch. III), and the preoccupation of the United States with the perilous situation in the Atlantic and Europe that blinded the nation to the menace of Japan in the Pacific until the very eve of open conflict. The next three chapters (VIII–X) relate the general plans and measures of the United States for defending Latin America against attack from overseas and for collaborating with the other American republics toward that end. The chapters which follow describe the specific steps in collaboration with Brazil (XI–XII), Mexico (XIII), and Canada (XIV–XV). The concluding chapter (XVI) is a summary and interpretation.

Key topics:

1. The background and development of war plans for defending the Western Hemisphere (Chs. I–II, IV–VII).

2. The relationship of these hemisphere defense plans to broader war plans (Chs. II, IV–VII).

3. The transition in national military policy from hemisphere to world defense against aggression (Chs. I–VII).

4. The nature and extent of German and Japanese threats to the American continents (Chs. III, V–VII).

5. Military negotiations and relationships of the United States with the other American nations before and during World War II (Ch. VIII).

6. The supply of arms to Latin American nations (Chs. IX, XI–XIII).

7. Preparations for Army air operations in the Latin American area (Ch. X).

8. The establishment and operations of U.S. Army forces in Brazil (Chs. XI, XII).

9. Military cooperation and collaboration between the United States and Mexico (Ch. XIII).

10. Military cooperation and collaboration between the United States and Canada

(Chs. XIV–XV; treated more fully in *Military Relations Between the United States and Canada: 1939–1945*).

11. U.S. Army operations in northern Canada during World War II (Ch. XV).

12. Army-Navy joint action and relationships in support of hemisphere defense plans and measures (Ch. I).

13. The interplay between military and political objectives in planning and executing hemisphere defense measures (Ch. I).

14. The organization and strength of the United States Army, 1939–41 (Chs. I–II, VI).

15. The military weakness of the United States during a period of rapid mobilization (Chs. II, IV–VI).

16. Army plans for emergency expeditionary forces (Chs. I, II, IV–VII).

17. American entry into the Battle of the Atlantic (Chs. I, II, IV–VI).

18. American military policy and plans for action toward European possessions under threat of hostile control (Chs. I, II, IV–VII).

19. The Destroyer-Base Agreement of 1940 (Ch. II).

20. Plans for military action in the Azores, Iceland, and other Atlantic areas during 1940 and 1941 (Chs. IV–VII).


**GUARDING THE UNITED STATES AND ITS OUTPOSTS.** By *Stetson Conn, Rose C. Engelman*, and *Byron Fairchild*. (1964, 1989; 593 pages, 5 tables, 1 chart, 6 maps, 34 illustrations, bibliographical note, glossary, index, CMH Pub 4–2.)

This volume continues the discussion begun in *The Framework of Hemisphere Defense* by describing how the Army contributed to the security of the national bastion. The discussion naturally divides itself into three sections. The first describes organization of Army forces for protection of the continental United States before and during the war, including elaboration of harbor and air defenses; the Army's role in civilian defense; and protection against subversion after Pearl Harbor, including a detailed account of the controversial evacuation of persons of Japanese ancestry from the West Coast. The next section outlines the Army's preparations for defense of the principal outlying possessions of Hawaii, Alaska, and the Canal Zone and includes an abbreviated account of the attack at Pearl Harbor and the Aleutian Islands Campaign, the only major ground operation to occur in the hemisphere during the war. The third section explains the creation of Army defenses to secure the Panama Canal in the south and the similar outpost line erected in the North Atlantic.

Governmental decisions to participate in the defense of Greenland and Iceland are explained as the culmination of American defensive measures by ground and air forces before the United States became a belligerent in World War II. Throughout, the authors stress the intimate relationship between American policy and the preservation of a North Atlantic lifeline to Great Britain, as well as the direct relationship between security of the Americas and the operations of the Royal Navy. Two other issues merit special mention. First is the tension between the natural desire to use a limited Army to defend the hemisphere in the opening days of the war and the need to use those same soldiers to train the large citizen army needed to pursue the war. Second is the evolution of the nation from a defensive to an offensive posture, specifically during the Coral Sea, Midway, and North Africa campaigns in view of the steadily declining threat of Axis attacks directed at the United States proper.

Key topics:

1. Transition from peacetime Army command and organization to wartime organization (Chs. II, III).

2. Problems in establishing unity of command among the services for hemisphere defense (Ch. IV).

3. The defensive problems facing the United States as a continental power isolated by two oceans, and the relationship between security of the homeland and offensive action in overseas theaters (Ch. III).

4. Defensive preparations in the outlying possessions of the United States during 1940 and 1941 (Chs. VII, IX, XII, XIII).

5. Acquisition, manning, and organization of new bases in the Atlantic and Caribbean in 1940–41 (Chs. XIV, XV).

6. Administrative processes leading to the administration's decision to evacuate resident enemy aliens and Americans of Japanese ancestry from the western states (Ch. V).

7. Fighting on the periphery of the American defensive perimeter in 1941–42, including Pearl Harbor, Alaska, and the Panama Canal Zone (Chs. VII, X, XI, XVI).

8. Establishment of wartime bases in Greenland and Iceland (Chs. XVII, XVIII, XIX, XX).

# The War in the Pacific

# The War in the Pacific

The volumes of the United States Army in World War II devoted to the war in the Pacific form a comprehensive account which should be of interest both to soldiers and civilians. Each volume is complete in itself and can be read independently. (Cross references guide the reader to other volumes for additional information.) The emphasis throughout is on the U.S. Army, but operations of the U.S. Navy, Air Forces, and Marines, as well as those of Allied nations, are covered in summary where they are related to the Army's operations or when they had an important or decisive effect on the outcome. The level of treatment and the amount of detail included vary with each volume and are determined by the nature of the operation. Each book includes sufficient material on strategy, logistics, and the activities of supporting arms and services to make clear why an operation was undertaken and how it was supported.

The plan of the Pacific subseries was determined by the geography, strategy, and the military organization of a theater largely oceanic. Two independent, coordinate commands, one in the Southwest Pacific under General of the Army Douglas MacArthur and the other in the Central, South, and North Pacific (Pacific Ocean Areas) under Fleet Admiral Chester W. Nimitz, were created early in the war. Except in the South and Southwest Pacific, each conducted its own operations with its own ground, air, and naval forces in widely separated areas. These operations required at first only a relatively small number of troops whose efforts often yielded strategic gains which cannot be measured by the size of the forces involved. Indeed, the nature of the objectives—small islands, coral atolls, and jungle-bound harbors and airstrips—made the employment of large ground forces impossible and highlighted the importance of air and naval operations. Thus, until 1945, the war in the Pacific progressed by a double series of amphibious operations each of which fitted into a strategic pattern developed in Washington.

In recognition of this fact, the Pacific subseries is organized chronologically by campaigns corresponding approximately to the divisions of command and to the strategical objectives set by the Joint Chiefs of Staff. First in the subseries (the volumes are unnumbered) is *The Fall of the Philippines* which describes fully the Japanese air attacks on the opening days of the war, the invasion that followed, the withdrawal to Bataan, the tragic defeat there and on Corregidor, the campaigns in Mindanao and the Visayas, and the final surrender in May 1942.

The next two volumes deal with the operations in the Solomons and New Guinea conducted simultaneously (August 1942–February 1943) but under separate commands.

*Guadalcanal: The First Offensive* describes the campaign in the Solomons by Admiral William F. Halsey, Jr.'s South Pacific forces; *Victory in Papua* details the long struggle of General MacArthur's Southwest Pacific forces to oust the Japanese from Buna on the southeast coast of New Guinea. Final success in these two campaigns in February 1943 removed the danger to the Allied line of communications running from the United States to Australia and prepared the way for an offensive against Rabaul, the great Japanese base in New Britain.

Neutralization and encirclement of that bastion were accomplished between June 1943 and March 1944 in a series of operations described in *CARTWHEEL: The Reduction of Rabaul*. These operations consisted of simultaneous and coordinated drives along the New Guinea coast and up the Solomons "ladder" by forces of the South and Southwest Pacific under MacArthur's direction. Included in the volume are accounts of the campaigns against New Georgia, Bougainville, Lae, Salamaua, Finschhafen, Cape Gloucester, and the Admiralties.

While the offensive against Rabaul was in progress, Admiral Nimitz's forces in the Central Pacific took the offensive and between November 1943 and March 1944 seized successively positions in the Gilbert and Marshall Islands (Makin, Tarawa, Kwajalein, and Eniwetok). These operations, described in *Seizure of the Gilberts and Marshalls*, advanced Allied forces 2,700 miles across the Pacific. Operations in the Marianas during the following June and July are covered in a separate volume, *Campaign in the Marianas*, which describes operations against Saipan, Tinian, and Guam, take-off point for the B–29 raids against Japan.

In the Southwest Pacific General MacArthur's forces, starting with the landing at Hollandia in New Guinea in April 1944, advanced by a series of amphibious hops up the New Guinea coast until by September they had reached Morotai, at the threshold of the Philippines. These operations, which include the seizure of Aitape, Wakde, Biak, Noemfoor, and Sansapor as well as the Central Pacific Campaign in the Palaus, are described in *The Approach to the Philippines*.

The liberation of the Philippines is described in two volumes. The first, *Leyte: The Return to the Philippines*, carries MacArthur's forces, augmented by a U.S. Army corps from the Central Pacific, into the heart of the archipelago in October 1944. From there, the troops of the Southwest Pacific went on to take Mindoro, Luzon, the Visayas, and Mindanao in a series of operations described in the volume entitled *Triumph in the Philippines*. The bulk of this volume deals with the recapture of Luzon, the most important island in the archipelago.

The forces of the Central Pacific, meanwhile, had continued their drive toward the Japanese home islands, capturing Iwo Jima in February 1945 (an operation not covered in this series since no Army troops were involved) and landing in the Ryukyus at the end of March. This last campaign, which went on until July, a month before the Japanese surrender, is described in *Okinawa: The Last Battle*.

A capstone volume, *Strategy and Command: The First Two Years*, views the background and progress of the war in the Pacific from the perspectives of Washington as well as of the theater commanders. It deals with the major strategic, organizational, and logistical plans and problems through December 1943 that affected U.S. Army operations in the Pacific and set the pattern for the war against Japan.

**STRATEGY AND COMMAND: THE FIRST TWO YEARS.** By *Louis Morton*. (1962, 1989; 761 pages, 13 tables, 16 charts, 17 maps, 92 illustrations, 23 appendixes, bibliographical note, glossaries, index, CMH Pub 5–1.)

This volume is the capstone of The War in the Pacific subseries, drawing on the operational volumes that preceded it in the subseries and providing the broad perspective on Japanese and Allied interests in the Pacific basin that shaped the war between these antagonists. As one of the later volumes in the United States Army in World War II series, it cross-references and often amplifies coverage of global strategic issues in the volumes on *Strategic Planning for Coalition Warfare* and *Global Logistics and Strategy*. Since this work traces the growing tensions between Japan and the United States against the broad background of prewar military planning, it also provides a useful complement to *Chief of Staff: Prewar Plans and Preparations*.

After sketching early U.S. strategic thinking about the problem of Pacific strategy, with special attention to the problems of defense of the Philippines, the work presents a full treatment of evolving Japanese strategy through the decision for war. Early Allied strategic decision, to include the "Europe First" policy, the challenges associated with accommodating U.S. policy to "colonial" and commonwealth expectations, and the tensions between the U.S. Army and the Navy are developed carefully. Steps taken at the national and coalition level during the early months of Japanese victories on vast fronts are presented in the context of the clashes of arms that resulted in those victories. After the fall of the Philippines, the Allied command relationships stabilized, and the various headquarters are described in detail as products of the complex political, geographic, and strategic factors that shaped them. Complementary sections analyze the Japanese command system, highlighting both its strengths and weaknesses.

Since the Pacific is clearly a joint theater, naval battles, Marine Corps contributions, and the myriad tactical questions that spill over into strategic debates are presented. Logistical difficulties abound in the theater selected for the "economy of force" effort, and the ways in which enemy action, bureaucratic decision making, and powerful personalities undermined the Europe First priority system provide useful lessons for those who are interested in problems in policy implementation.

After the battles of Coral Sea and Midway, both sides in the Pacific theater attempted to match resources with strategic concepts to impose their will on the enemy. The United States was hampered in this effort by a lack of unity of command, the vastness of the Japanese defensive perimeter, and the distances from U.S. ports. This volume traces the evolution of strategic plans designed to overcome those difficulties and outlines the operations conducted in consonance with those plans.

Throughout, the impact of the major conferences among the Allies that shaped their grand strategy of the war is assessed, and the twists and turns imposed on strategy by the actions of the enemy are described. Even though the volume ends with plans being evolved in late 1943, the material capabilities and doctrinal framework necessary to achieve tactical victory were in place by that time, and the strategic pattern for the remainder of the war was reasonably clear. The last six volumes of operational history in the subseries each contain the necessary strategic setting for the campaign described.

While focusing primarily on action in the Central and Southwest Pacific, this volume also provides the strategic setting for operations in the Aleutians covered in greater detail in *Guarding the United States and Its Outposts*. In this volume, as in all others, the detailed citations to the U.S. Navy's and U.S. Air Force's histories provide a fuller understanding of the campaigns in the Pacific theater.

Key topics:

1. Unity of command, combined and joint (Chs. XI, XVI, XXIV).

2. Planning and preparation for joint operations (Chs. XIX, XX, XXI, XXV).

3. Interplay among theater, JCS, and combined strategic concepts (Chs. VII, VIII, XI, XXIV).

4. Relationships between political and military considerations (Chs. II, III, IV, VII, IX, XXII, XXVII).

5. Divergence of strategic outlook of the Army and Navy (Chs. XI, XIII, XVI, XXII).

6. Relation between military planning and war aims (Chs. II, V, XVIII, XXII, XXIX).

7. Planning against scarce resources (Chs. XIV, XV, XXIII, XXVI).

8. War Department and Joint Board prewar strategic planning (Chs. I, II).

9. Evolution of the Europe First policy (Chs. II, III, XVIII).

10. Japanese High Command organization and decisions (Chs. IV, V, X, XVIII, XXVII).

11. Initial Japanese offensive (Chs. VI, VII, VIII, XII).

12. Initial Allied command relationships and defensive responses (Chs. VI, VII, VIII, IX, X, XI).

13. Army-Navy command relationships and theater-level joint planning (Chs. XI, XIII, XVI, XVII, XIX, XXIII, XXIX).

14. Planning and executing CARTWHEEL (operations in South and Southwest Pacific, August–December 1943) (Chs. XX, XXV, XXVI, XXVIII).

15. The Philippines and the Central Pacific strategy debate (Chs. XXII, XXIII).

16. The Aleutians in Pacific strategy (Ch. XXI).

**THE FALL OF THE PHILIPPINES.** By *Louis Morton*. (1953, 1989; 626 pages, 11 tables, 26 maps, 57 illustrations, bibliographical note, index, CMH Pub 5–2.)

This work treats one of the initial campaigns of the war of the Pacific (8 December 1941 through 6 May 1942), which ended with the Japanese conquest of the Philippine

Islands. The records of the victorious force, always better preserved than those of the vanquished, were at the disposal of the author, while those of the U.S. Army that survived have been supplemented with personal documents, letters, and extensive interviews. The result is a study of decisions and operations on each side of this campaign in relation to those of the other.

The first Philippine campaign presents an opportunity to study a retrograde movement by large American forces (the withdrawal to Bataan) and the methods by which General MacArthur and his commanders executed it with complete success. The book also recounts in detail the defeat and surrender of an American force of 140,000 men. It also presents the campaign in the larger perspective of global strategy and national policies, underlining the consequences of staking vital strategic and political objectives on military means insufficient to secure the objects of national policy.

The hope of holding the Philippines until the fleet could arrive was fading long before that fleet was crippled at Pearl Harbor. But the belief that long-range bombers in the Philippines could serve as a deterrent to the military expansion of the Japanese in Southeast Asia led the United States in July 1941 to place at General MacArthur's disposal all the B–17 bombers then available and in production. That illusion was destroyed and the Philippines virtually isolated when General MacArthur's air power was shattered on the first day of war. The present volume focuses new light on the heritage of controversy and conflicting explanations which that disaster produced.

The author's account of the subsequent campaign presents in detail a fight by American ground forces against an enemy in complete control of the air and sea. His book traces step by step the short-lived effort to stop the Japanese on the beaches, the withdrawal to Bataan, and the stubborn defense of Bataan and the island of Corregidor. The American forces, largely Filipino, were ably handled but were inadequately trained, ill equipped, and hastily mobilized. They included one infantry regiment of the U.S. Army and the 4th Marine Regiment. Their armament was of ancient vintage: the Enfield rifle, Stokes mortar, 2.95-inch mountain gun, .75-mm. and 155-mm. guns of European manufacture, and the light tank. The condition of Corregidor, Gibraltar of the Far East, illustrates vividly the effects of military obsolescence in armament and concepts of defense. In a real sense, the Philippine campaign was the last battle of World War I.

The logistical aspects of the campaign were of great importance and are fully developed in this volume. The long-standing ORANGE plan called only for defense of Corregidor and Bataan until the fleet could arrive in Manila Bay—a period estimated at six months. But Bataan had not been adequately stocked for a siege of this duration. Furthermore, General MacArthur, departing from the ORANGE plan, decided to oppose the enemy on the beaches. When this opposition immediately collapsed, supply officers had only two weeks to retrieve the stores they had brought forward and move them back to Bataan on crowded roads. Much had to be destroyed. The book gives a full account of the effect of shortages of supplies in producing the final agony of the troops and the decision by Maj. Gen. Edward P. King, Jr., to surrender in spite of direct orders of superior authority not to do so.

The reduction of Corregidor, Lt. Gen. Jonathan M. Wainwright's surrender, and its effect on the forces in the southern Philippines illustrate vividly the situation of commanders confronted with the unwelcome decision to surrender while still capable of effective local resistance. They also bring out with dramatic vividness the problems that face higher commanders confronted with defeat.

Key topics:

1. The effect of military unreadiness on a major strategic plan (ORANGE) (Ch. IV).

2. The capabilities and limitations of a force of non-American troops constructed around a trained American nucleus (Chs. VIII, X–XIII).

3. The defense of a beachhead by American forces (Chs. VI, VIII).

4. The effect of communications and command relationships under conditions of surprise (Ch. V).

5. Effects of enemy command of the air and sea on the control, tactics, and morale of an American force (Chs. IX, XXII, XXIV, XXV, XXVII, XXX).

6. The prolonged retrograde movement of a large force under strong pressure (Chs. XIII, XVI).

7. The prolonged defense of an extensive fortified position under conditions of siege, air attack, and supply shortages (Bataan) (Chs. XVI–XIX, XXIII–XXVI).

8. Defense of a heavily armed and fortified island under similar conditions (Corregidor) (Chs. XXVII, XXIX–XXXI).

9. The relation of logistical planning and the disposition of supplies to the capacity for resistance (Chs. IX, X, XV, XXI, XXII).

10. The problems of surrender (Chs. XXVI, XXXII).

11. The use of World War I weapons and tactics in the first American campaign of World War II (Chs. II, VIII, XI, XV, XVI, XVII, XVIII, XXVII, XXVIII, XXIX).

**GUADALCANAL: THE FIRST OFFENSIVE.** By *John Miller, jr.* (1949, 1989; 413 pages, 3 charts, 36 maps, 76 illustrations, 5 appendixes, glossary, index, CMH Pub 5–3.)

*Guadalcanal: The First Offensive* is a tactical history of ground operations involved in seizing and holding the heavily jungled island of Guadalcanal in the British Solomon Islands. It covers the campaign from the initial invasion on 7 August 1942 to 21 February 1943 when the area including the Russell Islands was finally secured. In the Pacific subseries this volume follows *The Fall of the Philippines,* is concurrent with *Victory in Papua,* and precedes *CARTWHEEL: The Reduction of Rabaul.*

The Guadalcanal Campaign was the first sustained Allied offensive in the Pacific. It began a series of amphibious attacks in the South and Southwest Pacific Areas which pointed toward the reduction of the great Japanese base at Rabaul in the Bismarck Archipelago. Just as the Japanese hoped to use Rabaul and their forward bases in the Solomons, the Bismarck Archipelago, and New Guinea to sever the U.S.-Australian line of communications, so the Allies planned their offensives to protect that line of communications and indirectly to clear the way for the return of American forces to the Philippines.

To seize the initiative from the Japanese, the Americans were initially forced to launch their offensive before they had amassed the preponderance of military strength that characterized the latter phases of the war. Japanese reaction was so violent and the contestants were so evenly matched on the sea and in the air that the campaign developed into a six-month struggle for control of the approaches to Guadalcanal coupled with intense ground fighting for possession of the island itself. While air and naval forces fought six full-scale naval battles and hundreds of smaller engagements, American ground combat troops grappled with Japanese military forces in the tropical rain forests, in the mountains, and on grassy hills. The fight was hard, and the enemy skillful and stubborn. Nevertheless, the final American victory demonstrated that their leadership, determination, tactics, and weapons were as effective in the damp dark of the jungle as in the desert or on the open plains.

The measure of the campaign is not to be found in the relatively small numbers of troops engaged. The Americans and Japanese were straining to bring their forces to bear at the end of long and vulnerable lines of communications, so that battalion and regimental actions assumed a much greater degree of importance than they did in, for example, the campaign in Europe during 1944 and 1945.

*Guadalcanal: The First Offensive* treats operations of U.S. Army ground combat troops in detail. It summarizes the achievements of U.S. Marine Corps, Navy, Air, and Allied units in order to show the contributions of all. Starting at the level of corps and division headquarters, ground combat is explained systematically down to the battalion level. When possible, key actions are carried down to the level of companies, platoons, and even squads, for combat in the thick tropical jungles tended to break up into a series of small-unit fights. Every attempt is made to show the contributions of all supporting arms and services, so that air, artillery, engineer, and signal support are related to infantry action as closely as possible.

Key topics:

1. A case study of the strategic problems facing the high (JCS) command: theater problems versus grand strategy (Ch. I).

2. An amphibious offensive: an early example of planning and execution (Chs. II, III).

3. Organizing beachhead defenses (Ch. IV).

4. The dependence of tactical strength on logistics (summarized in Ch. XIII; see also Chs. II–V).

5. Japanese offensive plans and operations (Chs. V, VI).

6. As others saw us: "Through Japanese eyes" (App. D).

7. Tactical subjects:

    a. The corps in the attack (Chs. XI, XII, XIV).

    b. The regiment in the attack, with artillery and air support (Ch. XI, Sec. 1).

    c. Attack of a heavily defended area (Chs. X, XII).

    d. Defense against Japanese attack (Chs. IV, V, VI).

    e. Employment of field artillery (Ch. XI, Sec. 1, and Ch. XII, Sec. 2).

    f. A hastily improvised attack (Ch. V).

**VICTORY IN PAPUA.** By *Samuel Milner*. (1957, 1989; 409 pages, 23 maps, 69 illustrations, bibliographical note, glossaries, index, CMH Pub 5–4.)

Soon after the shattered American Navy won its great victory at Midway, the United States launched its ground forces into their first offensives in the Pacific, at Guadalcanal as recounted above, and on the eastern tip of New Guinea. The offensive in Papua was an Allied operation in which the American ground contingent was supplied by two U.S. Army divisions, the 32d and a regiment of the 41st. *Victory in Papua* is a detailed account of their bitter experience in the operation to which they were committed, the objective of which was to expel the Japanese from their lodgments at Milne Bay, Buna, and Gona.

This was the first offensive under General MacArthur's command, and the American forces used were untried, neither trained nor seasoned for their difficult first assignment. For most of the Allied troops the Papua Campaign was a military nightmare. The work describes the agonies and frustrations of men living under almost intolerable conditions, plagued by disease, short of artillery, and pitted against a skilled and resolute foe.

While the narrative focuses on the painful struggles of the American ground forces to master their environment and overcome their foes, its scope is as broad as the campaign and includes the direction of joint, Allied operations; the operations of the Australians; and the sometimes highly experimental employment of air power to transport and supply the ground forces as well as support them in battle.

Key topics:

1. Problems of joint and Allied command (Ch. II).
2. Problems in theater strategy (Chs. I, II).
3. Japanese offensive plans and operations (Chs. I, III, IV, V, VI).
4. Air transport and supply (Chs. V, VII).
5. Improvisation of logistic support (Chs. V, VII, VIII, X, XI).
6. Effects of disease and insufficient training upon tactical efficiency (Chs. VII–XVIII).
7. Small-unit attacks against fortified areas (Chs. VIII–XVIII).
8. Special problems of command (Chs. X, XI).

**CARTWHEEL: THE REDUCTION OF RABAUL.** By *John Miller, jr.* (1959, 1984, 1990; 418 pages, 2 tables, 11 charts, 22 maps, 89 illustrations, bibliographical note, glossary, index, CMH Pub 5–5.)

The numerous and varied operations which resulted in the reduction of Rabaul illuminate Allied strategy, tactics, and command. The Allied offensive, begun with limited and costly counteroffensives on Guadalcanal and in eastern New Guinea, now began to take unexpectedly long strides. Postponement of the cross-Channel attack in favor of the invasion of North Africa, together with the rapidly mounting productivity of the American war economy, made it possible for the United States to deploy more strength in the Pacific in 1943 than its planners had originally anticipated. But Japanese strength had not yet been seriously impaired except in aircraft carriers, and Japan had the advantage of interior lines. The victorious operations that led to the isolation of Rabaul thus provide an inspiring and instructive story of successes won by strategic daring, tactical resourcefulness and flexibility, and human ingenuity and courage. They also demonstrate a remarkable capacity for teamwork at all levels. The Allied forces engaged, under the strategic direction of General MacArthur, were the ground, air, and naval surface forces of the South Pacific Area under the command of Admiral Halsey and those of the Southwest Pacific Area under the command of General MacArthur. Their ability to work and learn together was a remarkable achievement.

The operational strategy that grew into a pattern in this campaign called for ground forces, transported and protected by Allied naval and air forces, to seize bases from which the air forces and navy then neutralized other enemy bases in a continuous process of cooperation and forward leaps. To meet the enemy's determination to fortify heavily their advance bases and inflict high casualties in any attacking force, the Allied commanders used their superior strength to seize positions that were strategically important but weakly defended. Out of this emerged the bypassing technique whereby the Allies steamed or flew past strong enemy garrisons which were neutralized by air and naval action and left to wither on the vine. In the end, contrary to the original anticipations of the Joint Chiefs of Staff and General MacArthur, this method sufficed to dispose of the great enemy base at Rabaul.

CARTWHEEL provides information and references with which to study such variegated topics as Pacific strategy; intertheater relationships and coordination of widely separated forces and operations; problems and solutions in theater commands involving ground, air, and naval forces (U.S. and Allied); the relationship of such forces in a new pattern of warfare; and tactical problems and their solution, particularly in amphibious and jungle operations. The author also describes the close relationship of artillery, air, and naval support to infantry action wherever the records enabled him to do so and has been attentive to the relationship of logistics to progress in battle.

Key topics:

1. The execution of national strategy: a study in balancing ends against means (Chs. I, II, XII).

2. Theater headquarters in action: studies in unified command (Chs. III, VI, X, XI, XII, XIV, XV).

3. Intertheater cooperation and coordination (Chs. III, XII, XV).

4. Planning and executing amphibious offensives (Chs. V, VI, XII, XIV, XV).

5. Planning and executing a combined amphibious, overland, and airborne offensive (Ch. XI).

6. The corps in the attack (Chs. VIII, IX).*

7. The corps in defense, using interior lines (Ch. XVII).

8. The division in a jungle (heavy forest) attack, with emphasis on difficulties (Ch. VII).*

9. Operational techniques of bypassing strongpoints (Chs. X, XII, XV).

---

*These chapters also contain much material on operations of smaller units.

10. From reconnaissance in force to a divisional offensive (Ch. XVI).
11. Effective delaying action (Chs. VI–X).
12. Problems and solutions in jungle (heavy forest) warfare (Ch. IX).
13. War neurosis and combat fatigue (Chs. VII, VIII).
14. Japanese organization and strategy (Chs. IV, X, XI).


**SEIZURE OF THE GILBERTS AND MARSHALLS.** By *Philip A. Crowl* and *Edmund G. Love.* (1955, 1985, 1989; 414 pages, 4 tables, 3 charts, 27 maps, 92 illustrations, appendix, bibliographical note, glossaries, index, CMH Pub 5–6.)

This volume tells the story of the initial thrust in the drive across the Central Pacific. The campaign opened in November 1943 under Admiral Nimitz's direction, when the drive in the South and Southwest Pacific, directed by General MacArthur, was approaching Rabaul and was already on its way up the coast of New Guinea. Henceforth, a two-pronged offensive, coordinated by the Joint Chiefs of Staff, becomes the subject of the history of the war in the Pacific.

The decision to launch a double offensive against Japan revived the time-honored concept of a drive from Hawaii into the western Pacific, which had been laid aside, together with the ORANGE plan's focus on a Philippine offensive proved to be one of the momentous decisions in the war against Japan. A full account of the circumstances that lay behind this decision—the increase in American resources, the discussions at the level of the Joint and Combined Chiefs of Staff—appears in the volumes on *Global Logistics and Strategy* and *Strategic Planning for Coalition Warfare.* Its significance in Pacific strategy is further developed in the theater volume, *Strategy and Command: The First Two Years.* Here enough strategy is introduced to explain the two campaigns of the initial thrust under Admiral Nimitz.

In this first move only two Army divisions were engaged, the 7th and 27th. Their operations on Makin, Eniwetok, and Kwajalein are described and analyzed in detail, but the story of the whole operation, in which Navy, Marines, and Army Air Forces played the leading roles, is retold to the extent necessary to illuminate the decisions of Army commanders and present the action of the 7th and 27th Infantry Divisions in a historical context.

The operation was amphibious throughout because the islands seized were so small that naval forces provided essential gunfire and aerial support to the troops ashore until the end of the fighting. Once captured, these island groups (atolls) served as steppingstones in the form of advance air and naval bases from which future amphibious operations to the westward could be supported.

The present volume is particularly valuable as a study of the role of ground forces in amphibious operations. The errors made were instructive, and the lessons learned as well as the positions seized were an important contribution to the success of the subsequent advances, described in other Pacific subseries volumes. Specifically, the account contains instructive examples of the coordination of naval gunfire, artillery, and air strikes and the problems of successfully orchestrating a wide variety of ground, air, and sea components toward a unified purpose.

Key topics:
1. Strategic background of the campaigns (Chs. I, XXI).
2. Tactical planning for amphibious operations (Chs. II, III, XI).
3. Troop training for amphibious operations (Chs. III, XII, XIX).
4. Logistics of amphibious operations (Chs. III, XII).
5. Command relationships in joint (amphibious) operations (Chs. II, XI, XIX).
6. Amphibious landings against defended atolls (Chs. V, IX, XIV, XVIII, XIX).
7. Small-unit actions in atoll warfare (Chs. V, VI, VII, VIII, IX, XIV, XV, XVI, XVII, XVIII, XIX).
8. Naval gunfire support in amphibious operations (Chs. III, V, IX, X, XII, XIV, XV, XVI, XVII, XVIII, XIX, XXI).
9. Employment of artillery in amphibious operations (Chs. V, VI, VII, VIII, IX, X, XIV, XV, XVI, XVII, XVIII, XIX).
10. Air support in amphibious operations (Chs. III, V, IX, X, XII, XIV, XVIII, XIX, XX, XXI).
11. Tank-infantry coordination in atoll operations (Chs. V, VI, VII, VIII, IX, X, XIV, XV, XVI, XVII, XVIII, XIX).
12. Inapplicability of envelopment in small island tactics (Chs. V, VI, VII, VIII).
13. Underwater demolition teams in landing operations (Chs. XII, XIV).
14. Employment of amphibian vehicles in landing operations (Chs. III, V, IX, X, XI, XIV, XIX).
15. Japanese island defenses (Chs. IV, XIII, XIX).
16. Japanese counterattacks (Chs. VIII, IX, XVI, XIX).
17. Japanese strategy operations (Chs. IV, XIII, XIX).
18. Supply over the beaches in amphibious operations (Chs. VI, VII, IX, X, XIV, XVIII, XIX).

**CAMPAIGN IN THE MARIANAS.** By *Philip A. Crowl*. (1960, 1985, 1989; 505 pages, 2 tables, 2 charts, 34 maps, 89 illustrations, bibliographical note, glossaries, index, CMH Pub 5–7.)

*Campaign in the Marianas* tells the story of the capture of Saipan, Tinian, and Guam in the Central Pacific in mid-1944, together with the strategic and tactical planning that preceded the fighting, the supporting operations by air and sea forces, and the final exploitation of these islands as bases. The Marianas victory was one of the key actions in the Pacific; the U.S. invasion of the Marianas provoked the Japanese Fleet into a major and unsuccessful engagement, and the Marianas provided the bases from which the Army Air Forces later immolated the cities of Japan.

All Central Pacific operations shared certain characteristics. They were joint amphibious operations conducted under the principle of unity of command over all air, sea, and ground forces. They had as objectives potential air and naval bases which were to be seized by ground troops who were carried forward and supported by warships and airplanes. Their accomplishments involved hard fighting and relatively heavy casualties.

Because the number of Army troops in the Marianas was relatively small, much attention is devoted to small-unit actions, with the spotlight often falling on the rifle company. This account, like others in the Pacific subseries, also contains instructive examples of the coordination of naval gunfire, artillery, and air strikes, providing an exceptional opportunity to study the coordination of ground, air, and sea forces.

The Marianas invasions again demonstrated the soundness of U.S. amphibious doctrine and tested the principle of unity of command. This volume sheds light on interservice command and cooperation, treating frankly some of the bitter interservice controversies between the U.S. Army and the Marine Corps which emerged at the local level.

Key topics:

1. Strategic background of the operations (Ch. I).
2. Tactical planning for amphibious operations (Chs. III, XIII, XV).
3. Troop training for amphibious operations (Chs. III, XV).
4. Logistics of amphibious operations (Chs. III, VII, XV).
5. Command relationships and interservice cooperation and controversy in joint operations (Chs. III, VII, X, XV).
6. Amphibious landings on defended beaches (Chs. V, XVII).
7. Small-unit actions in island warfare (Chs. V, VI, VIII, IX, XI, XII, XVII, XVIII, XIX, XX).
8. Naval gunfire support in amphibious operations   (Chs. V, VII, XIV, XV, XVII).
9. Employment of artillery (Chs. VII, XII, XIII, XIV).
10. Air support (Chs. V, VII, XIV, XV, XVII).
11. Employment of amphibian vehicles in landing operations (Chs. V, XIII, XIV, XVII).
12. Japanese defenses (Chs. IV, IX, XIII, XVI).
13. Japanese counterattacks (Chs. VI, XII, XIV, XVII, XVIII).
14. U.S. and Japanese fleet operations (Ch. VII).
15. Movement of supplies over beaches in amphibious operations (Chs. V, VII, XIV, XVII).
16. Army versus Marine Corps (Chs. IX, X).

**THE APPROACH TO THE PHILIPPINES.** By *Robert Ross Smith*. (1953, 1984; 623 pages, 2 tables, 14 charts, 34 maps, 51 illustrations, bibliographical note, glossaries, index, CMH Pub 5–8.)

*The Approach to the Philippines* covers a series of seven complex amphibious and ground operations along the northern coast of New Guinea during the period April–October 1944, in the Southwest Pacific Area, and the capture of the southern Palau Islands, September–November 1944, in the Central Pacific Area. These operations paved the way for the Allied invasion of the Philippines in the late fall of 1944.

*The Approach to the Philippines* covers all activities—ground, air, and naval—necessary for adequate understanding of the Army ground narrative. The nature of combat usually involved a series of coordinated but separate operations by regimental combat teams. Divisions seldom fought as integral units during the approach to the Philippines.

The operations involved all the mechanics of amphibious warfare in 1944—strategic and logistical planning, naval gunfire, carrier-based and land-based air support, infantry maneuver, small-unit actions, artillery support, tank actions, tactical supply ashore, medical problems, and civil affairs. The series of operations described was unique, and the problems of execution involved were vastly complicated by the fact that they were executed in rapid succession. While one was being planned, another was being launched, the height of combat was being reached in a third, and still others had entered a consolidation stage.

Basically, *The Approach to the Philippines* becomes a story of joint operations from the highest to the lowest levels. Pertinent information about strategic planning by the Combined and Joint Chiefs of Staff is included to fit the tactical narrative into its proper perspective in the global war. At theater level the problems of joint planning, command, and organization for amphibious operations are covered in detail. At the tactical level may be found the story of a U.S. Army infantry company advancing along a coastal strand with the support of a U.S. Navy PT boat, while a fighter-bomber of the Royal Australian Air Force orbited overhead, ready to dive-bomb or strafe targets that the ground and naval units could not destroy. Or there is the story of a U.S. Navy destroyer and guns aboard amphibious craft manned by U.S. Army engineers that covered the withdrawal of an Army infantry battalion, while Army Air Forces planes protected all three elements. Finally, the plans and actions of the enemy are covered, principally from Japanese records.

Key topics:
1. Strategic planning, Allied and Japanese (Chs. I, IV, XV, XVIII, XIX).
2. Intelligence (Chs. II, VI, X, XII, XIII, XVII, XIX, XXII–XXIV).
3. Tactical planning for amphibious operations (Chs. II, IX, XII).
4. Logistical aspects of joint operations (Chs. II, III, V, XIX).
5. Organization for joint operations (Chs. II, IX, XIX).
6. Naval gunfire support (Chs. II, III, V, IX, XII, XIII, XVII–XXI).
7. Amphibious landings (Chs. III, V, IX, XII, XVII, XVIII, XX, XXI).
8. Assaults on defended islands (Chs. IX, XXI).
9. Defense of, withdrawal from, and reestablishment of a river line (Chs. VI–VIII).
10. Enveloping maneuvers in jungled terrain (Chs. III, VIII, XIII).
11. Cave and tunnel warfare (Chs. XIV, XVI, XXII–XXIV).
12. Air support, strategic (Chs. II, III, XVIII–XXI).
13. Tank operations, problems involved (Chs. III, X, XI, XIII, XIV, XXI–XXIV, XXVI).
14. Flamethrowers (Chs. XVI, XXII–XXIV).
15. Defense against naval counterattack (Ch. XV).
16. Army units under Marine Corps command (and vice versa) (Chs. XIX, XXI–XXIV).
17. Supply problems in roadless, tropical terrain (Chs. III, V, XIII, XIV).
18. Parachute operations (Ch. XVII).

**LEYTE: THE RETURN TO THE PHILIPPINES.** By *M. Hamlin Cannon.* (1954, 1987; 420 pages, 5 tables, 3 charts, 23 maps, 70 illustrations, 2 appendixes, bibliographical note, glossary, index, CMH Pub 5–9.)

In this narrative, the Sixth Army, commanded by Lt. Gen. Walter Krueger, emerges from the series of island-hopping, bypassing operations described in *CARTWHEEL: The Reduction of Rabaul* and in *The Approach to the Philippines* and engages a Japanese army on a land area of 2,785 square miles in a war of maneuver. The Sixth Army landed on Leyte on 20 October 1944 with the support of the fleets of the Pacific Ocean Areas and the Southwest Pacific Area, and these, in the famous Battle of Leyte Gulf on 24 October, blocked the desperate attempt of the Japanese Navy to destroy the expedition. U.S. Army troops were engaged in greater numbers than ever before assembled in the Pacific and were supported by naval and air forces of corresponding size. The Sixth Army had to overcome Japanese forces of greater magnitude than any previously encountered. On 25 December 1944, the island was declared secure, and General MacArthur returned in triumph to the Philippines. The breach in Japan's line of communications with Southeast Asia that had been effected by U.S. submarines was now permanent and its last hope of victory destroyed.

The Sixth Army accomplished its task on Leyte by executing a gigantic double envelopment coupled with an amphibious landing in the enemy's rear area. Throughout the campaign Krueger's army was aided by strategic and tactical air cover and support from its old companion, Lt. Gen. George C. Kenney's Fifth Air Force, and the Navy's air arm, and enjoyed the cooperation of guerrilla forces. The roles of supporting forces and strategic prospects and plans affecting the campaign are described to the extent necessary to explain the Army's plans and performance.

*Leyte* deals systematically with both American and Japanese operations. It gives an account of the plans and countermoves of the enemy, derived from Japanese sources. On the American side two corps and nine divisions were committed, and the study approaches operations from a corps and division level, but it amplifies the action of smaller units when those activities were particularly decisive or when available source material and space allowed the author to highlight the nature of the small-unit operations conducted.

The Leyte Campaign lasted longer than originally planned. In setting forth the circumstances of this delay *Leyte* illustrates the interdependence of ground and air forces. Although General Krueger officially assumed responsibility for the delay, the difficulty in constructing adequate airfields was the immediate culprit. The air forces were, for a considerable period, unable to seal off the battlefield, and the Japanese were able to funnel in reinforcements because the air bases on Leyte were not ready on time and were unsatisfactory when ready—a condition blamed on the soil, drainage, and climate of Leyte.

Key topics:

1. Logistical planning for an island campaign (Ch. III).
2. Relationships of ground, air, and naval forces in war (Chs. III, VI, XVI).
3. A large-scale amphibious operation: planning (Ch. III) and execution (Chs. IV–V).

4. Japanese command and strategy: a study in insufficiency, delay, and piecemeal commitment (Ch. IV, 3d section; Ch. VI; Ch. VII, 1st section; Ch. XVII; Ch. XXI, 3d section; this topic should be studied in conjunction with the Luzon Campaign).

5. Logistical problems in a tropical operation (Chs. XI, XVIII).

6. Mountain warfare (Chs. XII, XIII).

7. Exploiting an opportunity: an infantry division in amphibious envelopment (Ch. XVI).

8. A field army's summary of its tactical experience (Ch. XIV).

9. Kamikaze attacks (see Index).

10. Movement of supplies during the amphibious phase of an invasion (Ch. V, 4th section).

11. Guerrillas as a source of intelligence and employed in conjunction with regular troops (see Index: "Guerrilla movement").

**TRIUMPH IN THE PHILIPPINES.** By *Robert Ross Smith*. (1963, 1984, 1991; 756 pages, 9 tables, 45 maps, 87 illustrations, 8 appendixes, bibliographical note, glossaries, index, CMH Pub 5–10.)

*Triumph in the Philippines* is the third volume in the subseries to deal with the reconquest of the Philippine Archipelago. The narrative traces the broad strategic vision that was employed in arriving at the decision to invade Luzon and bypass Formosa as a steppingstone to Okinawa. This study focuses on the Luzon Campaign with twenty-nine of its thirty-two chapters devoted to this subject. Although the Pacific is decidedly a joint theater, the reader will find only passing references to naval activities in support of this campaign and will have to look to other sources for a more complete picture.

On 9 January 1945, the Sixth Army under the command of Lt. Gen. Walter Krueger commenced the largest United States Army operation in the Pacific. It entailed the use of more ground forces than did the operations in North Africa, Italy, or southern France. Unlike previous operations in the Pacific, the number of U.S. troops engaged, coupled with the ability to maneuver these forces in the central plains north of Manila, was more characteristic of European operations than any other Pacific campaign. By the time the campaign officially closed on 15 August 1945, over sixteen American divisions, or their equivalents, were committed to the liberation of the Philippines and the fulfillment of MacArthur's promise.

Starting with the landings at Lingayen Gulf, this volume traces the advance of the U.S. troops through the Philippine central plains and the recapture of Clark Air Base and Manila. The volume ends with U.S. troops in northern Luzon and the southern Philippines. Unusual for the Pacific theater are the operations associated with the capture of a major urban center, which proved to be more costly and destructive than originally estimated.

Accurate intelligence, always in short supply during hostilities, proved no less allusive in 1945. Throughout the campaign intelligence estimates between MacArthur and his field headquarters varied widely, affecting both strategic and tactical decisions. No where is this more evident than in the D-day estimate of Japanese strength on Luzon. Eight days after the invasion, the Sixth Army's original estimate of 152,500 defenders had been raised to 234,500, which proved closer to the Japanese actual strength of some 250,000. Continued overly optimistic assessments of Japanese strength eventually took its toll in American casualties and on morale during the seven and one-half months of campaigning.

When the war ended, General Yasmashita, the Japanese commander, was still conducting an active defense in northern Luzon with over 65,000 troops, estimated at the time by General Krueger to be no more then 23,000. Because of the surrender, large numbers of Japanese sources were available to the author, providing insight into the extensive Japanese dispositions, plans, and actions. The reader will find that due credit is given in this volume to the Japanese and their defense of the Philippines.

Key topics:
1. Assault of an urban center (Manila) (Chs. XIII–XVI).
2. Intelligence estimates during the Philippine campaign (Chs. II, X, XVIII, XXIX).
3. Use of armor (Chs. II, V, VI, IX, XI, XXIX).
4. Use of guerrillas in support of U.S. troops (Chs. XVII, XXII, XXV, XXVI, XXX, XXXI).
5. Use of tactical air to support ground operations (Chs. II, IV, XIII, XVII).
6. Airborne operations in support of the campaign (Chs. XII, XVII, XXIX).
7. Assault of heavily armed and fortified island positions (Ch. XIX).
8. Amphibious landings in the Philippines (Chs. II, IV, VI, XVII, XXII, XXXI).

**OKINAWA: THE LAST BATTLE.** By *Roy E. Appleman, James M. Burns, Russell A. Gugeler,* and *John Stevens.* (1948, 1984, 1991; 529 pages, 10 tables, 9 charts, 54 maps, 107 illustrations, 3 appendixes, bibliographical note, index, CMH Pub 5–11.)

*Okinawa: The Last Battle* is a tactical history of the conquest of the Ryukyu Islands by forces under the command of the U.S. Tenth Army in the period 1 April to 30 June 1945. The volume takes its name from the principal island of the Ryukyu island group, where the critical and decisive battles of the campaign were fought. The Ryukyus Campaign followed the capture of Iwo Jima and was planned as the last of the Pacific island operations before the invasion of Japan itself.

This work is an account of all United States forces engaged—Army, Navy, Air, and Marine. It also tells in considerable detail the story of the Japanese *32d Army*, which was the Okinawa garrison, and of Japanese naval and air forces committed in the defense of the Ryukyus. The volume begins with the planning for this amphibious operation at the threshold of Japan, one of the largest of the Pacific war, and follows the operation through all succeeding phases to the death of the Japanese commanding general and his chief of staff.

Of special interest was the tremendous volume of naval firepower employed by ships stationed offshore on the flanks of the American ground forces as the latter advanced across the island. The concentration of naval, air, and ground firepower employed by American forces in the Okinawa campaign was unparalleled for any comparable force, length of front, and duration of time in the history of warfare. Nevertheless, blunting this great firepower was the most extensive network of underground cave and tunnel defenses with tightly interlocking fields of fire encountered in the history of warfare. The Japanese defensive system stretched from coast to coast and converged ring upon ring in depth, with Shuri, the ancient capital of the Ryukyus, at its center.

The battle resolved itself into a myriad of small-unit actions against enemy cave and firing positions. This fight was conducted at close quarters by infantry-engineer and infantry-tank teams. Tank flamethrowers and engineer and infantry demolition teams, covered by small groups of riflemen, often formed the combat units that enabled Tenth Army slowly to destroy the many well-constructed defensive positions, eliminate their dedicated defenders, and move gradually forward. The extensive attacks of Japanese Kamikaze pilots against the American naval forces supporting the ground forces are also treated as an important part of the operation.

The ground combat story is told principally from regimental level. But as often as not, the treatment goes down to battalion level and frequently to company, platoon, and squad. It was the small unit that normally destroyed a particular enemy position holding the key to further advances. Often it was the individual soldier whose heroism was the decisive factor in such laborious activities, making it the theme of the immediate narrative.

The XXIV Army Corps and the III Amphibious Corps, U.S. Fleet Marine Force, were the principal subordinate units of Tenth Army. In the two corps were the Army's 7th, 27th, 77th, and 96th Infantry Divisions and the 1st and 6th Marine Divisions. In addition, the 2d Marine Division played a minor role in the preinvasion maneuvers, and its 18th Regiment was in limited action for a few days toward the end of the campaign.

Key topics:

1. The planning and conduct of a major amphibious operation (Chs. I, II).

2. Naval participation in an amphibious operation (Chs. I–III).

3. Establishment of beachheads on a hostile shore (Chs. III–VII).

4. Assault on a strongly defended small island (Ie Shima) (Ch. VII).

5. Attack and defense of a fortified line (Chs. V, VIII, IX, XI, XIII, XIV, XVII).

6. Attack of a fortified area (Chs. VIII–XV).

7. Small-unit tactics (Chs. V, VII, VIII, XI, XIII, XIV, XV, XVII).

8. Cave and tunnel defense (Chs. VIII, IX, XI, XVII).

9. Successful (enemy) withdrawal under attack (Ch. XV).

10. Naval gunfire support of operations ashore (Ch. VIII).

11. Employment of armor in broken terrain (Chs. V, VII, VIII, IX, XI, XIII, XIV, XVII).

12. Artillery (Ch. VIII).

13. Air support—Navy, Marine, and Army—much of it in close support of ground operations (see Index: "Air support").

14. Improvised use of weapons (Ch. X).

15. Supply (Ch. XVI).

16. Intelligence (Chs. IV, XV).

17. Influence of weather (rain) (pp. 360–82).
18. The relation of strategy and tactics (Ch. X).
19. Japanese defense:
    a. Organization and weapons (Ch. IV).
    b. Counterattack (Ch. XII).
    c. Kamikaze attacks (Chs. III, IV).
    d. Hara-kiri (Ch. XVIII).

# The Mediterranean Theater
# of Operations

# The Mediterranean Theater
# of Operations

This four-volume subseries begins with American troops, part of the Allied Expeditionary Force, wading through the surf on the beaches of Northwest Africa on 8 November 1942 and ends in the Italian Alps some 31 months later with the German surrender in May 1945. With supply lines always stretched to the breaking point, American and Allied soldiers faced a determined and resourceful enemy, harsh weather, inhospitable terrain, and indefinite goals in what many would later consider as little more than a sideshow to the "real" war in northern Europe.

Nevertheless, as these volumes trace the slow but steady advance of the Allies from North Africa, through Sicily, and up the Italian boot, the role that these campaigns played in wearing down the Axis powers and contributing to the final victory becomes evident. The authors also devote considerable attention to the politico-military negotiations leading to the surrender of the Italian Army, where military men were required to double as diplomats.

**NORTHWEST AFRICA: SEIZING THE INITIATIVE IN THE WEST**. By *George F. Howe*. (1957, 1985, 1991; 748 pages, 11 tables, 2 charts, 34 maps, 89 illustrations, note on sources, glossaries, index, CMH Pub 6–1.)

This volume is the history of the campaigns in World War II in which U.S. Army forces were first extensively engaged. It covers Operation TORCH, a massive amphibious, surprise assault in November 1942, after which the Allies speedily gained control of French Morocco and Algeria and obtained a toehold in Tunisia. It then describes the campaign in Tunisia which, beginning with stalemate in December 1942, involved broadening fronts, a buildup on both sides, concentration in Tunisia of Allied and Axis forces previously engaged in western Egypt and Libya, seesawing combat, and finally constriction of all Axis forces within northeastern Tunisia, where they surrendered en masse on 13 May 1943.

Other volumes of the United States Army in World War II also discuss TORCH. Its broader strategic connections are treated in *Strategic Planning for Coalition Warfare: 1941–1942*, and its effects on the logistical planning, resources, and capabilities of the Allies are taken up in *Global Logistics and Strategy: 1940–1943*. But it is here that the reader will find TORCH and the Tunisia Campaign described in their immediate political and military context. The author has drawn on abundant

German sources to illuminate the strategy and tactics of the enemy and produce a two-sided picture. Although primarily concerned with the role of U.S. ground forces, the narrative relates their efforts to the operations of sea and air forces of the several nations in both coalitions and takes into account the plans and operations by which the Allies wrested air superiority from the Axis.

The inexperienced ground forces of the United States were assigned holding or diversionary missions throughout the campaign in Tunisia. But they learned from experience, and in the final Allied drive in the spring of 1943 General Bradley's II Corps broke out of the mountains and occupied Bizerte at the same time that the British took Tunis.

*Northwest Africa* is a study of the trial-and-error process that characterized America's first large-scale campaign. It has unique interest as the narrative of the first invasion in World War II of territory held by a friendly nation, in which one objective of the Allies was to revive the military resistance of the French to the Axis conquerors. The planning and execution of TORCH were deeply conditioned by political considerations, and throughout both of the campaigns recounted in this volume the Allied command was ceaselessly confronted by difficult political issues along with those of a more strictly military nature.

Key topics:

1. Allied and Axis command structures compared (Chs. XIX, XXIV, XXV).

2. Tactical planning of joint task forces (Ch. III).

3. Problems of a successful command occupying colonial territory of a friendly nation (Chs. IX, XII, XIV).

4. Large-scale amphibious surprise assault on lightly defended shores (Chs. VI, VII, VIII, XI, XIII).

5. Offensive and defensive tactics along a broad front (Chs. XX–XXIV).

6. Establishing an integrated coalition headquarters (Ch. III).

7. Organized cooperation with the French on a clandestine basis (Chs. IV, X).

8. Defense of a mountain pass (Ch. XXIII).

9. Uncoordinated attacks and piecemeal commitment of forces (Chs. XXV–XXVII).

10. Rearmament of the French (Chs. XIV, XVIII, XXV).

**SICILY AND THE SURRENDER OF ITALY.** By *Albert N. Garland* and *Howard McGaw Smyth*. (1965, 1986, 1991; 609 pages, 17 maps, 113 illustrations, 4 appendixes, bibliographical note, glossary, index, CMH Pub 6–2.)

This volume describes the events surrounding the invasion of Sicily in July 1943 and the subsequent surrender of the Italian government. The book is divided into three sections. The first part sets the strategic stage by describing the debate between American and British strategists over the course of Allied operations in the Mediterranean theater during 1943. In recounting how the Allies came to agree upon the invasion of Sicily at the Casablanca Conference, the authors illustrate the difficulties of crafting grand strategy in coalition warfare. Additional aspects of the decision to invade Sicily and the interplay of Mediterranean operations with the proposed cross-

Channel invasion of France can be found in *Strategic Planning for Coalition Warfare: 1943–1944, Northwest Africa: Seizing the Initiative in the West*, and the two volumes on *Global Logistics and Strategy*. The problems of coalition warfare were not limited to the Allied side, however, and the book relates the difficulties the Axis experienced in formulating strategic plans and in defining command relationships. Part One of *Sicily and the Surrender of Italy* concludes with an analysis of Allied plans for the invasion of Sicily, code-named Operation HUSKY, and Axis defensive measures. In doing so, the volume highlights the challenges Allied planners faced in designing what was at that time the largest amphibious landing of World War II.

The second section of the present volume describes the invasion and conquest of Sicily—a rugged island bastion whose mountainous terrain greatly assisted the Axis defenders. The narrative fully examines the key Allied operational decisions of the campaign, including General Sir Harold Alexander's decision to shift the direction of the U.S. Seventh Army's advance, General George Patton's sweep to Palermo, and Anglo-American rivalry in the race for Messina. Axis actions on the island are also well documented. The book focuses, however, on the operations of the American Seventh Army. The combat narrative is written largely at the division and regimental level but occasionally dips down to individual companies in key combat actions. The type of operations described in the book include airborne and amphibious assaults, establishment and defense of a beachhead, mountain combat, and German rear guard tactics. Part Two of the volume culminates in the final Allied drive to Messina and the evacuation of Axis forces to Italy.

The invasion of Sicily sent shock waves through war-weary Italy and set in motion a movement that eventually toppled Mussolini from power. Part Three of *Sicily and the Surrender of Italy* returns to the strategic level, detailing the secret negotiations that eventually led to Italy's capitulation to the Allies, as well as Germany's countermeasures to seize control of the country. A discussion of the Allied decision to exploit the demise of fascism in Italy serves as a prologue for the next volume in The Mediterranean Theater of Operations subseries, *Salerno to Cassino*.

Key topics:

1. Strategic planning in coalition warfare, including the debate between the advocates of a "peripheral" strategy and a cross-Channel attack; the decision to invade Sicily; the Casablanca, TRIDENT, and Quebec conferences; and the question of how to exploit the collapse of Italy (Chs. I, XIV, XXI).

2. The erosion and ultimate dissolution of the Rome-Berlin Axis (Chs. II, XIV, XV, XXIV–XXIX).

3. Planning and organizing a large-scale, joint and combined invasion against a defended coast (Operation HUSKY) (Chs. III, V).

4. Negotiations for the surrender of Italy (Chs. XXII–XXIX).

5. Evolution of invasion plans (Chs. III, V).

6. The first major Allied airborne operation of World War II (Chs. VI, VII, IX, XXI).

7. Allied amphibious operations (Chs. VI, VII, XVIII, XX, XXI).

8. Modifying a campaign plan during the course of operations (Chs. XI, XII, XIII).

9. Challenges posed to U.S. forces by mountain warfare and German defensive techniques (Chs. XVI, XVII, XVIII).

10. The successful Axis evacuation of Sicily (Chs. XIX, XXI).

11. Difficulties in strategic and tactical surface-air coordination (Chs. V, IX, XXI).

12. Efforts to deceive the Axis about Allied invasion plans (Chs. III, IV).

13. Patton and the slapping incident (Ch. XXI).

**SALERNO TO CASSINO.** By *Martin Blumenson.* (1969, 1988; 491 pages, 16 maps, 94 illustrations, 2 appendixes, bibliographical note, glossary, index, CMH Pub 6–3.)

In September 1943 a combined British and American amphibious force finally made the first Allied landing on the continent of Europe. After campaigns which began with amphibious assaults in both Africa and Sicily, the Allies were hoping that the invasion of Italy would be an equally successful endeavor. Although the Italian capitulation on the eve of the invasion filled the troops with confidence that enemy resistance would rapidly collapse, the Allied campaign in Italy was as tough as any fought in World War II; if anything, the Italian surrender hardened German resistance. *Salerno to Cassino* begins the story of the Allied effort to wrest control of Italy from its German occupiers, while *Cassino to the Alps* provides the conclusion.

The confrontation in Italy was the first time Allied armies faced the German Army in a sustained campaign on the European mainland. During the first eight months covered by this volume the fighting was brutal and the situation on both sides was anything but optimistic. The opponents faced the same difficult terrain and bad weather and shared similar supply problems. The Germans, defending in the south, had their long supply lines subjected to the ever-increasing Allied air power, and the Allies had a chronic shortage of practically all types of shipping.

Although the author focuses on the tactical activities of the Allies with special emphasis on the U.S. Fifth Army, he also provides the strategic framework within which those activities took place. The account includes the German point of view and sketches of air and naval activities pertinent to understanding the ground situation. Highlights of the volume include the problems faced by American forces in the initial landings at Salerno, the difficulties encountered while attempting to force a crossing of the flooded Rapido River, the controversial decision to bomb the historical Benedictine abbey on Monte Cassino, and the stalemate at the Anzio beachhead.

Key topics:

1. Amphibious assaults (Chs. III, IV, VI, VII, VIII, XX).
2. River crossings (Chs. XII, XIII, XVIII, XIX).
3. Assaulting fortified towns (Chs. X, XVI, XXI, XXV).
4. Mountain warfare (Chs. XII, XIII).
5. Small-unit tactics (Chs. X, XII, XIII, XVI, XVIII, XIX, XXI, XXIV).
6. Use of air power (Chs. XIV, XXIII, XXIV).
7. German command problems (Chs. V, XI, XIV, XX, XXIV).
8. Strategic decision making in coalition warfare (Chs. I, X, XI, XIV, XVII, XXVI).

9. German defensive tactics (Chs. XIII, XV).
10. Use of airborne troops (Ch. VIII).
11. Coalition command considerations (Chs. IX, XXIV).

**CASSINO TO THE ALPS.** By *Ernest F. Fisher, Jr.* (1977, 1989; 584 pages, 27 maps, 92 illustrations, appendix, bibliographical note, glossary, index, CMH Pub 6–4.)

This volume continues the story of the Italian campaign with the Allied spring offensive in May 1944 which carried two Allied armies—the U.S. Fifth and the British Eighth—to Rome by 4 June and to the final German capitulation in May 1945. Represented in these armies were Americans, Belgians, Brazilians, British, Canadians, Cypriots, French (including mountain troops from Algeria and Morocco), Palestinian Jews, East Indians, Italians, Nepalese, New Zealanders, Poles, South Africans, Syro-Lebanese, and Yugoslavians. The Fifth Army also included the U.S. Army's only specialized mountain division, one of its two segregated all-black divisions, and a regimental combat team composed solely of Americans of Japanese descent.

The campaign involved one ponderous attack after another against fortified positions: the Winter Line, the Gustav Line (including Monte Cassino), and the Gothic Line. It called for ingenuity in employing tanks and tank destroyers over terrain that severely restricted the use of mobile forces. In addition the Allied attackers constantly had to devise new methods to supply forces fighting through dangerous mountain terrain in central Italy or those fighting in flooded lowlands along the Adriatic coast.

It was also a campaign replete with controversy, as might have been expected in a theater where the presence of many nationalities and two fairly equal partners imposed considerable strain on the process of coalition command. Among the most troublesome questions was the judgment of American commander, Lt. Gen. Mark Clark, to focus on the capture of Rome rather than conforming with the wishes of his British superior who was more concerned with trapping the retreating German forces. Other issues have proved equally controversial. Did Allied commanders conduct the pursuit north of Rome with sufficient vigor? Indeed, should the campaign have been pursued all the way to the Alps when the Allies might have halted at some readily defensible line and awaited the outcome of the decisive campaign in northwestern Europe?

Just as the campaign began on a note of covert politico-military maneuvering to achieve the surrender of the Italian forces, so it ended in intrigue and secret negotiations for a separate surrender of the Germans in Italy. Nevertheless, the 570 days which the Allies battled in Italy made it the longest sustained Allied campaign of World War II. The narrative ranges from detailed descriptions of company-level tactics up through division, corps, and army with considerable tactical detail at each level of command.

Key topics:

1. Grand strategy from both Allied and German points of view, including opposing command structures, and operational planning at army, corps, and division level, both Allied and German (Chs. I, II).

2. Corps operations in mountainous terrain (Chs. III, IV).

3. Planning for and breakout from a beachhead under enemy observation (Chs. VI, VII, VIII).

4. Mountain warfare, including classic stratagem for breaking through mountain defenses, the use of trained mountain infantry in a flanking maneuver, and the penetration of mountain passes (Chs. X, XXIV, XXVI).

5. Pursuit operations on a two-army front (Ch. XIII).

6. Armor in rugged terrain (Chs. XIII, XIV).

7. River crossings on a broad front (Ch. XXVIII).

8. Surrender negotiations (Ch. XXX).

9. Artillery support (see Index: "Artillery").

10. Operations in adverse conditions of weather and soil (mud, cold, rain, and floods) (see Index: "Floods; Mud; Terrain; Weather").

# The European Theater
# of Operations

# The European
# Theater of Operations

What and how three and one-half to four million Americans contributed to victory in the European Theater of Operations (ETO) during World War II is told in the ten volumes of the European subseries of the United States Army in World War II. These volumes are histories of units, commanders, headquarters, planning, decisions, strategy, tactics, and logistics. Because the end purpose of all activity in the theater was—as always in war—to close with the enemy and destroy him, a majority of the volumes deal with tactical operations. Yet armies without overall direction are little more than armed mobs: one volume thus tells the story of the Supreme Headquarters and the man who provided direction. Nor can a field army function without equipment, personnel replacements, supplies, or transport: two volumes tell this story.

The limits of the individual tactical volumes in this subseries were fixed according to well-defined phases of the operations in the ETO, rather than by arbitrary dates. Though an individual volume may deal with one or more armies in a given area at a given time, it contains adequate background and corollary information for understanding the place of these particular operations in the larger context. The influence of theater strategy, logistics, and adjacent combat operations is integrated into each story. Thus, each volume is an entity that can be read separately with profit; at the same time each takes a natural place in the framework of the whole.

Because the war in Europe was an Allied effort, the tactical operations of the British, Canadians, French, and other Western Allies have been sketched or summarized to place the American role in more realistic perspective. Every effort has also been made to avoid a nationalistic slant and to present fairly the critical problems of the grand alliance as revealed in planning and execution of strategy and operations. Nevertheless, it has not been possible, nor was it intended, to develop in full the narrative of Allied participation. Based largely on U.S. records, these volumes inevitably are written from an American point of view.

As these books are focused on the American role, so also are they a history of United States ground operations rather than sea and air. The reader is constantly made aware, nonetheless, that the sister services were vital parts of a team. Where air and naval matters directly affected policy or operations in the theater, this material is retained. In particular, the campaign volumes develop the role of tactical air forces as they affected fighting on the ground.

The story would be far less instructive without the corresponding picture from the enemy side. By study of interrogations and personal narratives of German officers, of captured documents, and of military records surrendered upon termination of hostilities, an accurate, interrelated account of enemy plans and operations has been developed to a degree not common in previous histories of this kind.

In the campaign volumes, attention has been focused, of necessity, on combat formations actually in the line. Nevertheless, the vital combination of arms and services essential to victory has not been overlooked. The verity and necessity of this combination are emphasized by the volumes on the supreme command and logistics. The basic unit of the narrative in the campaign volumes varies, depending on the scope of the particular volume. Usually it is the division whose story is told in terms of regiments and battalions.

*The Supreme Command* was designed as the capstone of the subseries. A history of Supreme Headquarters, it covers Allied Expeditionary Force (SHAEF) theater command and the Supreme Commander focusing on the nature of coalition command and the critical decisions made. Tactical operations at army group level are discussed, covering the entire war from D-day to V–E Day. In addition, more attention than in other volumes is given to political or nonoperational questions: civil affairs, press relations, military government, and so forth.

*Cross-Channel Attack* introduces the subseries providing background for study of all the campaigns in the European Theater of Operations. The volume focuses on planning of OVERLORD; D-day, the Normandy invasion; and tactical operations to 1 July 1944, when the Allies were assured of the success of the OVERLORD invasion, the fruition of plans and preparations reaching back as far as January 1942.

*Breakout and Pursuit* covers the "Battle of the Hedgerows" leading to Operation COBRA and victory in Normandy. The Falaise-Argentan pocket and the Mortain counterattack are also included, as are operations in Brittany, the reduction of Brest, and liberation of Paris. The volume closes with the pursuit across northern France and Belgium by the U.S. First and Third Armies, ending in early September at the German frontier and the gates of Lorraine.

*The Lorraine Campaign* chronicles the U.S. Third Army's struggle through the slow, arduous campaigning of the fall of 1944, from the Moselle to the German border and the West Wall in the Saar region. After the reduction of Metz, the story ends on 18 December when the Third Army was diverted to move against the German winter counteroffensive in the Ardennes.

*The Siegfried Line Campaign* parallels the effort in Lorraine, following the U.S. First and Ninth Armies during the fall of 1944 through similar costly fighting. The narrative takes the readers from first crossings of the German border on 11 September to the enemy's counteroffensive, which ended the campaign abruptly inside Germany along the Roer River on 16 December. Highlighted are piercing the West Wall, the reduction of Aachen, the bitter fighting in the Huertgen Forest, and the operations of the First Allied Airborne Army in Operation MARKET-GARDEN in the Netherlands. American participation in opening Antwerp and clearing the Peel Marshes is also included.

*Riviera to the Rhine* focuses on the ANVIL/DRAGOON amphibious assault in southern France on 15 August 1944 and thereafter covers the tactical operations of the 6th Army Group (Seventh U.S. and First French Armies) until February 1945. The initial lodgment, the pursuit up the Rhone valley, and winter warfare in the Vosges are all highlighted, as are the German *NORDWIND* offensive and the reduction of the Colmar Pocket.

*The Ardennes* treats the German winter counteroffensive in Belgium and Luxembourg. The volume covers the operations of the U.S. First and Third Armies from the start on 16 December 1944 to 3 January 1945, when successful elimination of the "bulge" was assured.

*The Last Offensive* chronicles the operations of all five U.S. armies from early 1945 to V–E Day. Special attention is given to Operation GRENADE and the sweep to the Rhine; the seizure of the Remagen bridge; the multiple crossings of the Rhine; and the employment of airborne troops in Operation VARSITY. The story ends with the drive to the Elbe and juncture with the Soviets and, in the south, with the occupation of Germany's Alpine Redoubt.

*Logistical Support of the Armies*, 2 volumes, is the keystone rather than the capstone of the subseries. Relating the story of the campaigns and the decisions of higher commanders to the tyranny which logistics exercises on their conduct, it discusses tremendous materiel buildup in the United Kingdom preceding D-day, the logistical aspects of the invasion, and the effect of pursuit warfare on the Allied logistical structure. *Volume I* ends with the termination of pursuit in mid-September 1944, while *Volume II* carries the story to V–E Day.

**THE SUPREME COMMAND.** By *Forrest C. Pogue.* (1954, 1989; 607 pages, 11 tables, 9 charts, 16 maps, 64 illustrations, 7 appendixes, bibliographical note, glossaries, index, CMH Pub 7–1.)

This book, while it contains the history of the Supreme Headquarters, Allied Expeditionary Force, is focused on the decisions of the Supreme Commander rather than the machinery of command. It is primarily a history of the decisions of General of the Army Dwight D. Eisenhower.

To present these decisions in the round, it includes their background: the situations, military and political, that confronted the Supreme Commander; the discussions leading to his decisions; and the controversies—inter-Allied, interservice, personal, or purely military—which he had to resolve. It also includes an account of the reactions to his decisions and their effect on the course of the war. Since the author drew his information and impressions from interviews with more than a hundred of the leading participants as well as from public and personal records, he has been able to assess and illustrate, in many cases, the weight of personality as a factor influencing Eisenhower's final decisions and their effect. To give further perspective, the author has drawn on German records and interrogations to present the enemy's views, plans, and positions, not always known to the Supreme Commander at the time.

The period covered runs from December 1943 to 14 July 1945. The author reaches back (in Ch. II) to review the origins of SHAEF and to summarize (in Ch. V) the evolution of General Eisenhower's strategic mission as embodied in the OVERLORD plan.

The volume deals with the most complex combined (Allied) and joint (Army, Navy, Air) command that had appeared in the history of war, a headquarters founded on the principle of Allied "integration," first applied by General Eisenhower in his organization of the Allied headquarters in the Mediterranean in 1942 (AFHQ). It was the culminating expression of the principle of unity of command which the Allies applied in World War II with varying degrees of success in all theaters of operations.

Recognizing this, the author has included the facts and references necessary for a study not only of the antecedents, machinery, and activities of SHAEF (Chs. II–IV), but also of its relations, on the one hand, with the Combined Chiefs of Staff, the supreme instrument of the Allied governments for the military direction of the war, and, on the other, with the principal subordinate commands that directed operations in northwestern Europe on land and sea and in the air, from 6 June 1944 until 7 May 1945.

The Supreme Commander's primary responsibility was military, and after 2 September 1944 he assumed direct command of the operations of the ground forces of the Allies. In order to furnish the setting and trace the consequences of General Eisenhower's military decisions, the book includes a full account of the campaigns of the Allied Expeditionary Force. The scale of this account is determined by the outlook of SHAEF. In general, it follows at army and army group level operations that are being recounted in greater detail in the campaign volumes of the United States Army in World War II and in the British and Canadian official histories. Since the present account is necessarily based chiefly on American records, it gives a more complete and authoritative history of American than of British operations.

Although the Supreme Commander's primary responsibility was military, the scope of his command repeatedly put him astride the traditional line between military and political considerations which modern war tends to obliterate. This line presented a problem in his relations with the British and French commanders, particularly with Field Marshal Sir Bernard L. Montgomery, and in the recommendations he had to make on relations with the Soviets in the last phase of the war. The volume also discusses in detail the difficulties of making politico-military decisions without timely, clear, or positive directives from higher authorities.

Key topics:

1. The planning and preparations for a vast inter-Allied surprise assault on a strongly defended coast and for pursuit and defeat of the enemy (Chs. V–VII, IX). (The plans and preparations here sketched are treated in more detail in *Cross-Channel Attack*.)

2. Command decisions at the highest level of Allied authority below the Combined and Joint Chiefs of Staff (see Index: "Eisenhower, General of the Army Dwight D.; Strategy, Allied").

3. The interplay between the views and decisions of the Joint and Combined Chiefs of Staff and those of the Supreme Allied Commander in the field, a treatment which supplements that given in the strategy and logistics volumes of the United States Army in World War II (see Index: "Combined Chiefs of Staff; Joint Chiefs of Staff; and Eisenhower, General of the Army Dwight D.").

4. Unity of command, combined and joint (Chs. II, III, VII, XV; see Index: "Command").

5. The mechanism and operations of a headquarters based on the principles of

command unity and integration (Ch. IV).

6. The tendency to create the large and complex headquarters characteristic of American military organization in World War II (App. B).

7. The interplay of military and political considerations in directing a command of this type (Chs. II, VI, VIII, XII, XIII, XVIII).

8. The campaigns of 1944–45 in France, the Low Countries, and Germany, at army group and army level, including the plans and operations of the enemy (Chs. X–XII, XIV, XVI, XVII, XX–XXIV). In this aspect the present volume is the capstone for the histories of American operations and logistics in the European theater subseries of the United States Army in World War II and, in a more limited degree, for the history of British, Canadian, and French operations.

9. Military government and the military administration of civil affairs, in military operations involving relations with a number of liberated countries and the occupation of enemy territory on the basis of unconditional surrender (Chs. IV, VIII, XIII, XVIII, XIX).

10. The controversies of General Eisenhower and Field Marshal Montgomery over strategy and command (see Index: "Eisenhower, General of the Army Dwight D., Montgomery's relationship with").

11. The surprise achieved by the Germans when they attacked in the Ardennes on 16 December 1944, and the countermeasures by which General Eisenhower and his principal commanders contained the attack and regained the initiative (Ch. XX).

12. The decision of General Eisenhower to halt his forces short of Berlin (Ch. XXIV).

13. Psychological warfare (Chs. IV, XIX).

14. Public relations of SHAEF (App. A).


**CROSS-CHANNEL ATTACK**. By *Gordon A. Harrison*. (1951, 1989; 519 pages, 4 charts, 31 maps, 62 illustrations, 10 appendixes, bibliographical note, glossaries, index, CMH Pub 7–4.)

The cross-Channel attack launched on 6 June 1944 under the direction of Supreme Headquarters, Allied Expeditionary Force, is a subject that reappears in many volumes of the United States Army in World War II, since it involved the U.S. Army in its most important and largest single undertaking in the war. This basic account of the attack is focused on the Army's participation in it, both as a plan and as an operation. It relates the project of the assault from its inception in 1942 to the strategic and logistical planning of the United States and the Allies (Chs. I–III) and to the plans, strength, and position of the enemy in 1944 (Chs. IV and VII); it describes the complex plans and preparations for the assault (Chs. V and VI), then narrates the fighting of the First Army to establish a lodgment up to 1 July 1944 (Chs. VIII, IX, and X).

Much of the book (seven out of ten chapters) is devoted to planning and preparations since this volume is intended to serve as an introduction to all of the campaigns of the U.S. Army in the European Theater of Operations, as described in Chapters VIII–X and in the other nine volumes of the ETO subseries.

Other volumes in the United States Army in World War II which devote considerable attention to the cross-Channel attack are *Washington Command Post: The Operations Division; The Supreme Command; Logistical Support of the Armies, Volume I;* and the volumes on *Strategic Planning for Coalition Warfare.* Detailed narratives of the assault on 6 June and the subsequent campaign to 1 July can be found in *Omaha Beachhead* (1945), *Utah Beach to Cherbourg* (1947), and *Small Unit Actions* (1946), all in the Army's American Forces in Action series. These narratives concentrate on the action of small units in combat.

*Cross-Channel Attack*, like most other campaign volumes in the ETO subseries, focuses on the division as the basic fighting unit, although it often describes in considerable detail the experiences of battalions and companies on the fragmented fields of Normandy. So far as enemy records permit, it tells the story of German action at the same level. *The Supreme Command*, on the other hand, deals with D-day and the campaign to establish the Normandy beachhead and capture Cherbourg, from the point of view of General Eisenhower and Supreme Headquarters.

Key topics:

1. An amphibious assault on a defended shore by a coalition force (for particulars, see items that follow).

2. The BOLERO concept (Chs. I–III; see Index: "BOLERO").

3. Early plans for the invasion of Europe from England: SLEDGEHAMMER (1942) and ROUNDUP (1943) (Chs. I–III).

4. The Anglo-American debate over a cross-Channel attack (Chs. I, III, V).

5. General Morgan's COSSAC and the evolution of the OVERLORD plan (Ch. II).

6. The conversion of OVERLORD into a dated plan of operations (Ch. V; for a digest of the OVERLORD plan, see App. A; for the Supreme Commander's directive, see App. B).

7. The contribution of enemy weakness to Allied success (Chs. IV, VII, X).

8. German command organization in the West (Ch. IV).

9. Hitler and the German defense against the invasion of Normandy (see Index: "Hitler" and Apps. C and D).

10. D-day on sea and land and in the air (Ch. VIII).

11. Securing a beachhead and lodgment area (Chs. IX–X).

Among the more specific topics on which this volume throws light are the following:

12. Debate on the ANVIL plan (Ch. V).

13. Organized cooperation of the French Resistance with the Allies (see Index: "French Resistance").

14. Effect on strategy of shortage in a critical item (landing craft) (see Index: "Landing craft").

15. Effect of a scattered airdrop (Ch. VIII).

16. Assault and capture of a fortified city (Cherbourg) (Ch. X).

17. Use of mass air-bombing and artillery in this assault (Ch. X).

18. Amphibious assault (see Index: "Amphibious tactics"):

    a. Naval fire support (see Index: "Naval fire support").

b.  Air-bombing of coastal defenses (plans, pp. 194ff.; execution, Ch. VIII).

c.   Mass use of airborne forces to effect "vertical envelopment" of a beachhead (see Index: "Airborne assault").

d.   Weather as a factor in planning an amphibious assault (see Index: "Weather").

e.  Defense at the beach line versus use of mobile reserves in meeting an amphibious assault (Ch. VII).

f.  Use and effect of communications bombing in isolating the battle area (Chs. VIII–X).

g.  Capabilities and limitations of underwater obstacles in defending a coast against assault (see Index: "Obstacles").

h.  Use of swimming tanks in the assault of a defended beach (see Index: "Tanks,  DD").


**BREAKOUT AND PURSUIT**.  By *Martin Blumenson*.  (1961, 1984, 1990; 748 pages, 34 maps, 93 illustrations, 2 appendixes, glossary, bibliographical note, index, CMH Pub 7–5.)

This volume follows the U.S. First and Third Armies from 1 July 1944 in the Allied sweep across France to the German border, where *The Siegfried Line Campaign* takes up the story of the First Army (on 11 September) and *The Lorraine Campaign* that of the Third Army (on 1 September). The present volume includes the battle for Brest, which ended (on 18 September) when the front had been pushed across France and beyond.

By 1 July the Allies had consolidated a firm beachhead which included Cherbourg and left no doubt that their armies had come to stay. The theme of the book is their subsequent efforts to acquire the "lodgment area" projected in the OVERLORD plan (see *Cross-Channel Attack*); the effort of the Germans to contain them; the breakthrough beginning on 25 July; its conversion into the breakout; the encirclement of German forces; and the ensuing sweep across France that outran all plans and anticipations.

After an explanation of Allied and German situations (Part One), the battle narrative opens (Part Two) with an examination of the hedgerow fighting—the costly and disheartening battles in the compartmentalized fields of Normandy which, combined with rain, mud, and inexperience, deprived the Americans of the advantages of numbers and mechanization in the offensive and assisted the Germans in their stubborn defense. The volume gives special attention to the methods by which the Americans overcame the unexpected difficulties that beset them and became experienced veterans.

The next phase of the narrative (Part Three) includes an account of the genesis and evolution of General Bradley's breakthrough plan (COBRA) and follows in detail the measures and events that marked its conversion into a triumphant breakout into Brittany (described in Part Four). The author then (in Part Five) recounts the swiftly changing plans of the Allies as they seized the opportunity to break out toward the east;

describes Hitler's counterattack toward Avranches and its defeat; follows (in Parts Six and Seven) the development of operations designed to encircle the Germans at Argentan and Falaise; and shows the fast-moving mobile warfare that characterized the drive to the Seine, the liberation of Paris, and the sweep to the borders of Germany. A tightening logistical tether (see *Logistical Support of the Armies, Volume I*) and the resuscitation of German resistance subsequently brought the First and Third Armies face to face with the bitter campaigning described in *The Siegfried Line Campaign* and *The Lorraine Campaign*.

The battle narrative in this volume is, in general, pitched at corps level, but the focus of attention moves up and down the chain of command to illuminate decisions, both Allied and German, at critical moments of the campaign. The action is carefully related to the declared or postulated intentions of the responsible commanders, and success or failure is examined with reference to these and the opposing moves of the contestants. As in *Cross-Channel Attack*, the access of the author to abundant enemy sources has made it possible for him to represent fully the strength, intentions, and tactics of the enemy.

Key topics:

1. Multiple crossings of a defended river line on a division front (Chs. V, XXVIII).

2. Assault of a fortified city (St. Malo, Ch. XXI; Brest, Ch. XXX).

3. Problems of coalition warfare on tactical levels (Chs. X, XXV–XXVIII, XXIX, XXXII).

4. Infantry:
    a. In compartmentalized hedgerow terrain (Chs. IV, V, VII, VIII, XIII, XV).
    b. In mobile warfare (Chs. XXVIII, XXXI, XXXII).
    c. In achieving a breakthrough (Chs. XII–XIV, XXVII).
    d. In defense (Chs. VII, VIII, XIV, XV).

5. Armor:
    a. In hedgerow terrain (Ch. VI).
    b. In a breakthrough (Chs. XIII–XVI, XXVII–XXIX).
    c. In mobile warfare (Chs. XIX, XX, XXVIII, XXXI, XXXII).
    d. The armored division as an independent striking force (Chs. XIX, XX).

6. Air support:
    a. Use of heavy (strategic) bombers in direct support of ground troops (Ch. XII).
    b. Tactical air support of ground operations (Chs. XII, XIII).

7. Artillery in special situations:
    a. Under infantry attack (Chs. XV, XVI).
    b. Against fortress defenses (Chs. XXI, XXX).

8. Commitment of inexperienced units and their errors (Chs. IV, V, VI, VIII, XV).

9. Logistics of mobile warfare (Chs. XXVIII, XXX–XXXII).

10. Effect of weather on tactical air (see Index: "Weather, effect on operations").

11. Traffic congestion and its effect on operations (Chs. XVI, XIX, XXVIII).

12. Personnel replacements (Ch. XI).

13. Use of task forces for unusual missions (Chs. XXI, XXX).

14. Artillery support (see Index: "Artillery support").

15. German command problems (Chs. II, XVII, XXIV, XXVII).

**THE LORRAINE CAMPAIGN**. By *Hugh M. Cole*. (1950, 1984; 657 pages, 50 maps, 67 illustrations, bibliographical note, glossaries, index, CMH Pub 7–6.)

This volume narrates the operations of the U.S. Third Army, commanded by Lt. Gen. George S. Patton, Jr., during the autumn of 1944 when that army was weakened by a lengthy pursuit and taut supply lines and faced an enemy who was rapidly recovering behind strong natural and artificial barriers. The iron hand which logistics sometimes imposes on tactical operations is in evidence throughout the narrative. Like other operational volumes dealing with the European theater, *The Lorraine Campaign* is organized into chapters at corps level and written primarily at division level. When action at a lower level was decisive or particularly illustrative, the narrative descends to regiment, battalion, company, and sometimes to platoon and squad level. Concurrent operations of Allied and of other U.S. armies are sketched in as necessary for a complete understanding of the Third Army's story. Companion volumes recount in full the concurrent campaigns of the First and Ninth Armies (*The Siegfried Line Campaign*) and of the Seventh Army (*Riviera to the Rhine*). The story of command and decision at levels higher than army headquarters is told only where it had a direct bearing on the fighting in Lorraine, as, for example, General Eisenhower's decision to halt the Third Army at the Meuse River at the start of September while he concentrated his strained resources in support of the First Army on another axis of advance (Ch. I).

Despite General Patton's long-lived optimism that he could gain the Rhine in one quick thrust, this volume indicates that even in early September the Germans were amassing strength sufficient to delay an overextended attacker for a long time behind such barriers as the flooded Moselle River; the historic forts ringing Metz, capital of Lorraine; and the Maginot and Siegfried Lines. This is the story of the slow, plodding operations that developed in the forests and among the rolling hills of Lorraine from early September until the Third Army on 18 December was turned north to assist the First Army in the Ardennes.

A parallel account from the enemy side puts the American operations in proper perspective. The volume contains also an analytical description of the decisions of commanders at army, corps, and division levels that provided the framework of the tactical operations. Historical perspective is enhanced by frequent reference to earlier campaigning over this same terrain in 1870, 1914–18, and 1940.

Key topics:

1. Multiple crossings of a defended river line on an army front (Chs. II, III, VIII).

2. Assault of a fortified city (Metz) (Chs. III, VI, VIII, IX).

3. Assaults of strongly fortified lines—Maginot (Ch. X) and Siegfried (Ch. XIII)— in the latter case a line behind a river.

4. Tank fighting:

    a. Against a counterattack in force (Ch. V).

    b. In an army offensive (Chs. VIII, X).

    c. In the assault of a fortified line (Ch. XII).

(Note: b. and c. are examples of armor operating under adverse conditions of weather and soil trafficability.)

    5.  Street fighting (Chs. VIII, IX).

    6.  Air support of ground operations (see Index: "Air support").

    7.  German armor versus American (Ch. XIV; for German armor, see also "Panzer formations" in Index under "German units").

    8.  Armored task forces in limited objective attacks (see especially Ch. VII).

    9.  Artillery support (see Index: "Artillery").

    10.  Engineer (see Index: "Bridges; Engineer") and smoke generator units in support of river crossings. (For a more detailed account of the Moselle crossing at Arnaville, see *Three Battles: Arnaville, Altuzzo, and Schmidt*.)

    11.  Operations in adverse conditions of weather and soil (mud, cold, rain, and floods) (see Index: "Floods; Mud; Terrain; Weather").

    12.  Forest fighting (see Index: "Woods fighting").

    13. Command problems: German (see Index: *"OB WEST;* Oberkommando der Wehrmacht [OKW]").

**THE SIEGFRIED LINE CAMPAIGN**. By *Charles B. MacDonald*. (1963, 1984, 1990; 670 pages, 19 maps, 81 illustrations, 4 appendixes, bibliographical note, glossaries, index, CMH Pub 7–7.)

    Optimism ran high when the first American patrols crossed the German frontier on 11 September 1944. With the enemy defeated in Normandy and pursued across northern France, Belgium, and Luxembourg, who could doubt that the war in Europe would soon be over? As events were to prove, and as this volume relates, buoyant spirits were premature. Aided by the concrete of the Siegfried Line (the so-called West Wall) and the forbidding terrain along the frontier, the Germans were able to stabilize the front against an Allied force weakened by the excesses of a long pursuit.

    *The Siegfried Line Campaign* is primarily a history of tactical operations in northwestern Europe from early September to mid-December 1944. It covers in detail the campaigns of the U.S. First and Ninth Armies and the First Allied Airborne Army and in sketchy outline the concurrent operations of the Second British and First Canadian Armies. Organized into chapters at the corps level, the story is told primarily at division level with numerous descents to regiment and battalion and even at times to lower units. Logistics and high-level planning (for example, the controversy over single thrust versus broad front strategy) are treated where they affected the campaign. Discussion of staff operations at army or corps level is limited to the development of tactical plans and operations.

    Although the First Army's V and VII Corps both penetrated the Siegfried Line in September, ragtail German formations were able to blunt these spearheads. They did the same when the Allies sought to outflank the West Wall by crossing three major water barriers. The last of these, an assault on the lower Rhine, was a major coalition operation that combined the First Allied Airborne Army attack in southeastern Netherlands (Operation MARKET) with a ground attack (Operation GARDEN) by the Second British Army. From this point (late September) stiff in-fighting developed. Into November the Allies in Belgium, Germany, and the Netherlands conducted a series of small-scale operations to tidy the front in preparation for another major attempt to break through to the Rhine River and encircle the Ruhr industrial area. They focused on several specific missions: capture of Aachen, which sits astride the invasion route to the Ruhr; a drive on the Huertgen Forest southeast of Aachen to protect the forces before Aachen and to capture the dams on the upper Roer threatened by the retreating Germans; and reduction of the German bridgehead west of the Maas River in southeastern Netherlands. The Allies also sought to clear the seaward approaches to Antwerp, whose port remained the key to the logistical problems that had plagued them since the Normandy breakout.

By mid-November Allied commanders could report considerable success in these missions. Greater strength had been added with the introduction of the Ninth Army into the line between the First Army and the British. The logistical situation was gradually improving, and in conjunction with the Third Army to the south, the First and Ninth Armies were preparing a new offensive designed to carry all three to the Rhine.

Operation QUEEN was launched on 16 November, but by taking advantage of their strong artillery reserves, the inclement weather, and rough terrain, the Germans slowed the advance significantly. By mid-December some Allied troops had not traversed the seven miles to the intermediate objective of the Roer River, and the threat of the Roer Dams still existed. Coincidentally, the Germans used the time to mobilize behind the front an army group that would launch a counteroffensive in the Ardennes, bringing a halt to the Siegfried Line campaign.

Key topics:

1. Attack and defense of a fortified line (Chs. III, IV, VIII).
2. Forest, city, and village fighting (Chs. IV, XIII, XIV, XV).
3. American units under foreign command (Ch. IX).
4. Armor operations (Chs. XI, XXII).
5. Airborne operations (Chs. VI, VII, VIII).
6. Air support of ground troops (Chs. IX, XII, XVII, XVIII, XIX).
7. Success and failure in intelligence estimates (Chs. XI, XXIII).
8. Fighting in inclement weather (Chs. II, III, VIII, XVII).
9. Comparison of American and German tanks (Ch. III).
10. Use of smoke, searchlights, flail and flamethrowing tanks, M–29 cargo carriers, tank track, and connectors (grousers) (Chs. XXIV, XXVI).

**THE ARDENNES: BATTLE OF THE BULGE.** By *Hugh M. Cole.* (1965, 1983; 720 pages, 14 maps, 93 illustrations, 2 appendixes, bibliographical note, glossary, index, CMH Pub 7–8.)

This volume deals with the great German offensive in the Ardennes and Schnee Eiffel during December 1944; the armored drive to isolate the Anglo-Saxon Allies by the seizure of Antwerp; and the defensive battles fought by units of the U.S.

First, Third, and Ninth Armies reinforced by troops from the British 21 Army Group. *The Ardennes: Battle of the Bulge* opens with the detailed planning and preparations in the German headquarters (Chs. I, II, IV) and follows the development of the campaign from the surprise attack initiated on 16 December to the point where, in the first days of January 1945, the Allies regained the initiative and resumed the offensive to cross the Rhine. The discussion parallels that given in the latter sections of *Riviera to the Rhine*, covering the southern Allied Army Group, and sets the scene for *The Last Offensive*.

The Ardennes, as in other volumes of this subseries, is structured on the division as the chief tactical and administrative unit. However, in the early hours and first days the battle mandates that the story be told at platoon and company level with cross reference to battalions, regimental combat teams, and armored combat commands. Command and control exercised by the army corps generally appears in the allocation of reserves rather than in tactical direction of the battle. Higher command efforts come into the narrative in a few specific instances, such as the gross failure of Allied intelligence; the geographic division of command between Montgomery and Bradley; the decisions to hold the American linch-pins on the Elsenborn ridge, St. Vith, and Bastogne, at the shoulders of the German salient; and the initial large-scale counterattack mounted by the Third Army. (The subject of command is given close analysis in *The Supreme Command*.)

The history of German command and troop operations is told in considerable detail. At the close of World War II, German officers were brought together so as to re-create the commands and general staffs of the major units taking part in the Ardennes campaign. As a result of this exercise in collective memory *The Ardennes* has an unmatched wealth of precise and parallel information on "the other side of the hill." Much attention is also given to the role played by the Allied air forces—particularly the tactical air commands—and to the effect of weather on air-ground cooperation and on German logistics.

The story begins with the irruption of enemy assault units in force against the green 99th and 106th Infantry Divisions and throughout the breadth of the thinly held VIII Corps front. The German breakthrough in the Schnee Eiffel is given detailed attention (Ch. VII). There follows the American attempt to narrow the rapidly evolving enemy salient by hard fighting at the shoulders of the bulge and by piecemeal tactical reinforcement at these critical points. The exploitation phase of the German offensive sees early armored successes interspersed with delays and halts inflicted by isolated and lone American combined arms detachments plus the vagaries of weather and terrain. This combination of adverse weather and difficult terrain is analyzed as it influenced German armored operations and conditioned the assault or the defense at barrier lines, roadblocks, and timbered patches (Chs. VI, XIV). The tactics of perimeter defense are shown in the record of battles at Bastogne (Ch. XIX) and those in the ring around St. Vith (Chs. XII, XVII).

This volume concludes with the final desperate effort of German armor to reach and cross the Meuse River; with the stiffening American defense at the leading edge of the salient, coupled with the German failure to widen it at the shoulders; with the commencement of the enemy withdrawal; and with the counterattacks of the Third and First Armies. The final episodes of the Ardennes battle are recounted in *The Last Offensive*.

Throughout this volume the strictures imposed on German maneuver by logistical failures are evident as are the superior American capability to reinforce and resupply the defense. (See also *Logistical Support of the Armies, Volume II*). Nonetheless, the German campaign to keep rail and road transport functioning, here described in detail (Ch. XXV), merits close study.

Key topics:

1. Elementary tactics as shown in the many episodes of "the starkness of small unit combat" (Foreword; Chs. VI, VII, VIII, IX).

2. Mobile operations under adverse conditions of weather, terrain, and short daylight hours (see Index: "Mud; Terrain"; Ch. XXV).

3. Organization, tactics, control, and communications in delaying actions (see Index: "Mud; Tactical control; Communications, problems").

4. Failure of Allied intelligence (Ch. IV).

5. Ad hoc air resupply (see Index: "Air supply").

6. The employment of combat engineers (see Index: "Bridges; Bridging operations; Engineers; Barrier lines; Obstacles"; Ch. XIV).

7. Tactical surprise by maneuver, through operations at night and in the fog, and by the use of smoke and deceptive lighting (see Index: "Surprise, tactical").

8. Examples of a double envelopment (Ch. VII).

9. Detailed description of the employment of "the combined arms" (see Index: "Task Forces; Teams").

10. Tanks; antitank combat (see Index: "Tanks; Armor; Mechanized forces").

11. Tactical air support (see Index: "Aircraft, fighter-bombers"; Ch. XXV).


**RIVIERA TO THE RHINE**. By *Jeffrey J. Clarke* and *Robert Ross Smith*. (1992; approx. 620 pages, 1 table, 35 maps, 77 illustrations, bibliographical note, index, CMH Pub 7–10.)


On 15 August 1944, the Allies finally launched Operation ANVIL, code name for the amphibious assault against southern France. Long in the planning as an adjunct to the main effort in Normandy, the effort represented a victory for U.S. strategists seeking to focus Allied military strength against western Germany. The successful assault was rapidly followed up by the seizure of the important French Mediterranean ports of Marseille and Toulon and a concerted drive north up the Rhone River valley to Lyon. There the Franco-American Riviera Force, consisting of the U.S. Seventh and the French First Armies, was combined into the Sixth Army Group under Lt. Gen. Jacob Devers as the southern element of General Eisenhower's northern European command.

From September to November 1944 the Sixth Army Group struggled east through the Vosges mountains and through the Saverne and Belfort gaps to the north and south, respectively. Inclement weather, rugged terrain, and stiffening defense by the German *Nineteenth Army* slowed the army group's progress toward the German border to a crawl. During the well-planned November offensive, however, Devers' forces surged through the German lines, rapidly advancing to the Rhine and destroying the cohesiveness of the defenders in the process. But rather than move directly into Germany, Eisenhower ordered the bulk of the Seventh Army to strike northward in support of the U.S. Third Army's less successful offensive in Lorraine. In the process the Army group lost its momentum, allowing the Germans to retain a foothold in the Vosges around the city of Colmar and in the north to conduct a more orderly withdrawal to the German border.

In December the German Ardennes offensive forced the Sixth Army Group to halt all offensive operations and extend its front northward. As a result, the German High Command launched Operation *NORDWIND* in January 1945, a major armor and infantry offensive against the extended Seventh Army. A stubborn but flexible defense finally wore the German forces thin, but both sides suffered heavily from the bitterly cold weather. In February, Devers' forces resumed the offensive, eliminating the Colmar Pocket and the *Nineteenth Army* and setting the stage for the final drive into Germany.

This volume links the U.S. Army's Mediterranean and northern European operational series together and provides an important counterpoint for those works dealing with Eisenhower's two more well-known army groups commanded by Field Marshal Sir Bernard Montgomery and Lt. Gen. Omar Bradley. The opening section (Chs. I–XI) treats the Southern France Campaign as part of the Mediterranean Theater of Operations; a middle section (Chs. XII–XXIV) covers the fighting in the Vosges; and the final section (Chs. XXV–XXX) takes up the battle of Alsace. Joint operations are highlighted (Chs. II–VII) in the treatment of ANVIL, perhaps the most successful amphibious operation during the war, while the problems of combined (multinational) command are discussed throughout. A full account of German plans, organization, and actions is included for perspective, and the operations of the First French Army, a major component of the American army group, are also treated in detail.

Key topics:

1. Combined and joint politico-military war planning (Chs. I, II, XII, XXVII).

2. Partisan guerrillas (Chs. III, VI).

3. Amphibious loading for logistics (Ch. III).

4. Air-sea-land interdiction operations (Chs. V, VI).

5. Armored warfare (Chs. IX, XXI, XXIII, XXVIII, XXIX).

6. Civil affairs (Ch. XI).

7. Close air support (Ch. XI).

8. River crossings (Chs. XIII, XXII).

9. Morale and discipline (Ch. XXX).

10. Special and airborne operations (Chs. III, VI).

11. Winter and mountain fighting (Chs. XV, XXIX).

12. Intelligence derived from communications intercepts and human sources—ULTRA and the OSS (Ch. V).

**THE LAST OFFENSIVE.** By *Charles B. MacDonald.* (1973, 1984, 1990; 532 pages, 27 maps, 92 illustrations, 2 appendixes, bibliographical note, glossaries, index, CMH Pub 7–9.)

*The Last Offensive* is the final volume of the United States Army in World War II subseries The European Theater of Operations. It recounts the closing battles in which the American forces cross the Rhine River—historic boundary of German power—and, with the Western Allies, defeat and destroy Hitler's armies deployed on the Western Front. The story in these final chapters follows those told in *The Ardennes: Battle of the Bulge* and in *Riviera to the Rhine*; the time frame extends from the first days of January 1945 to V–E Day (8 May).

The massive force under Eisenhower's command had attained the battle experience of a professional army; it was superior to the *Wehrmacht* both in manpower and materiel. On V–E Day Eisenhower would have under his command more than four and a half million troops: 91 divisions (61 of which were American), 6 tactical air commands, and 2 strategic air forces. In this volume appears a reckoning of the total Allied effort in the West and the human cost accumulated between D-day and V–E Day. In these months a total of 5,412,219 Allied troops had entered the European Theater of Operations, along with 970,044 vehicles and 18,292,310 tons of supplies. Allied casualties for the period of combat are estimated at a figure of 766,294. American losses are carried as 586,628, of which 135,576 are listed as dead (Ch. XX).

*The Last Offensive* is a dramatic piece of military history and offers a varied array of ground force operations. In these final months the U.S. First, Third, Seventh, and Ninth Armies, reinforced by British and Canadian armies on the northern flank and a French army on the southern wing, erased the two German salients west of the Rhine (in the Ardennes and around Colmar) and drove to the long-time Allied objective, the Rhine. The powerful assaults to force the Rhine crossings were accompanied by a prime example of "luck" in battle, the seizure of the Remagen bridge, and abetted by a spectacular air-drop assault Operation VARSITY—the last of the war (Ch. XIV). Beyond the Rhine there follows a series of the most massive sweeps and wide turning movements in World War II, engulfing and destroying the German armies in the Ruhr Pocket (Ch. XVI). The end of the *Wehrmacht* comes when the Americans join the Soviets at the Elbe (Ch. XVII) while the Seventh U.S. Army races to and crosses the Danube (Ch. XVIII).

The gigantic size of these operations requires that this volume be structured with emphasis on the army but with close scrutiny of important engagements by divisional organizations. The detailed story of the Allied command in this period will be found in *The Supreme Command.* Nonetheless, *The Last Offensive* analyzes the controversy between Eisenhower and Montgomery over the competing strategies based on an advance all along the front versus a narrow, deep, and powerful thrust on a very constricted front. Here it is shown that the Allied front expands from 450 miles in January to twice that width at V–E Day. Also, explanation is given herein regarding Eisenhower's decision to halt the advance of the Western Allies on the Leipzig axis, short of Berlin. Despite the great Allied superiority on the ground and in the air, the war weary and weakened German troops fought stubbornly in these last battles; *The*

*Last Offensive* gives credit to these veteran troops fighting in a hopeless and meaningless cause.

Key topics:

1. The "grand tactics" of wide encircling sweeps and deep penetrations (see Index: "Armor, exploitation").

2. Tactical and technical problems in the crossing of defended rivers and the consolidation of bridgeheads (see Index: "Rhine; Roer; Moselle"; Ch. XI).

3. Effect of varied combinations of terrain and weather on mechanical operations (see Index: "Tanks; Weather").

4. Management of logistics in support of rapid movement by large forces (see also *Logistical Support of the Armies, Volume II*).

5. Organization for combat at the division level during operations of deep penetration and rapid exploitation (see Index: "Divisions *by number*").

6. Tactics and techniques of bridging and assault craft operations at large water barriers (see Index: "LVTs; DUKWs; Boats, assault; Bridges; Engineers, bridging operations").

7. Tactical use of smoke, fog, and weather (see Index: "Smoke; Weather").

8. Airborne transport and vertical encirclement by air (Ch. XIV).

9. Air interdiction in support of Allied ground operations (Ch. XIV).


**LOGISTICAL SUPPORT OF THE ARMIES, VOLUME I: MAY 1941–SEP-TEMBER 1944.** By *Roland G. Ruppenthal*. (1953, 1985, 1989; 616 pages, 11 tables, 6 charts, 18 maps, 58 illustrations, bibliographical note, glossaries, index, CMH Pub 7–2.)

This is the history of the logistical operations in the European Theater of Operations in support of the U.S. Army forces in that theater from 1941 to mid-September 1944. The operations described and analyzed were under the direction of the headquarters of the combined command known as ETOUSA Communications Zone. But the focus throughout is on the relation of logistics to combat and the influence of adequate or inadequate logistical support on the planning and conduct of tactical operations by the field armies. Two major problems of supply that had important effects on these operations are treated in detail: the shortage of gasoline in the period of pursuit and the developing shortage of field artillery ammunition, which became critical in the fall of 1944.

Beginning with the arrival of the first small group of U.S. Army "Special Observers" in May 1941, the narrative tells the story of the successive predecessor commands in the United Kingdom and the activation of the European theater (Ch. I). It covers in turn the buildup of forces and logistical planning in preparation for the cross-Channel invasion (Chs. II–VII) and then logistical operations on the Continent through the end of the phase of rapid pursuit in September (Chs. X–XIV).

The major theme is logistical difficulties, first those of building up U.S. forces for the invasion of France, then of supporting them in combat. For the period of continental operations emphasis centers largely on problems of movement: cross-Channel shipping, the development of beach and port discharge facilities, and long-distance transportation by rail and truck, including the famed Red Ball Express (Ch. XIV).

Full attention is given to theater organization and command, particularly to the relation of logistics to other functions, and to the influence of personalities on the evolution of command and on administrative effectiveness (Chs. I, II, III, V, and XI).

Key topics:

1. Logistical (OVERLORD) planning for large-scale offensive operations (Chs. IV, VII).

2. Theater command and territorial organization, particularly where an Allied command is superimposed on a national command and a single commander holds positions in both (Chs. I–III, V, XI).

3. The influence of logistical considerations on tactical planning and decisions (Ch. XII).

4. Manpower problems, particularly with respect to economical use of personnel, and the variance of casualty experience of the first months from estimated replacement needs (Ch. XI).

5. The logistics of rapid movement and its effects on future capabilities (Chs. XII–XIV).

6. Competition between global and theater strategy and priorities in the buildup of supplies and forces (Chs. II, III, VI).

7. Supply over beaches in support of a large invasion force, including the use of artificial ports (Chs. VII, X, XI).

8. The influence of personalities in the development of theater organization and in the relationship of theater commands to each other (see especially Ch. XI).

9. The results of inadequate planning and staff coordination in meeting urgent calls for logistical support (Ch. XIII).

10. The development of a theater troop basis (Ch. III).

11. Early struggles attending the establishment of a U.S. Army command in the United Kingdom (Ch. I).

12. Relations with an ally which serves as "host" nation and on which U.S. forces must depend heavily for locally procured services and supplies (Chs. II, III, VI).

13. Effect of the North African invasion on the preparation of a force in the United Kingdom for the cross-Channel invasion (Ch. II).

14. Training and rehearsing for the cross-Channel attack (Ch. VIII).

## LOGISTICAL SUPPORT OF THE ARMIES, VOLUME II: SEPTEMBER 1944–MAY 1945. By *Roland G. Ruppenthal.* (1959, 1983; 540 pages, 14 tables, 11 maps, 65 illustrations, bibliographical note, glossaries, index, CMH Pub 7–3.)

This volume moves from mid-September 1944 to the end of hostilities in May 1945 along the same general lines as *Volume I* described above. As in that volume the focus is on the influence of adequate or inadequate logistical support on the planning and conduct of tactical operations by the field armies, in short, the relation of logistics to combat. Considerable space is given to theater organization and command because of the influence that these exerted on effective administration and support.

The main divisions of the volume correspond to the two broad phases of tactical operations in the period covered: the period of relatively static warfare from mid-September 1944 to early February 1945 (Chs. I–XII) and the period of offensives leading to the surrender of Germany in May 1945 (Chs. XIII–XVIII). The main topics examined within each period are organization and command (Chs. II, XII, XIII, XIX); port discharge (Chs. III, IV, XIV); transportation (Chs. V, VI, XIV, XV); supply (Chs. VII, IX, XVI); and manpower (Chs. XI, XVII).

The reader will find (in Ch. I) an assessment of the logistical basis of General Eisenhower's decision in September 1944 against concentration of his resources on a single thrust to the Rhine. In Chapter XII the author surveys, in the light of the Somervell-Lutes "tour of inspection" in December 1944–January 1945, the structure of theater administration and supply as tested by the logistical problems encountered between D-day and the Ardennes offensive of mid-December. The book concludes with general observations on the logistical experience of the European theater (Ch. XIX).

*Logistical Support of the Armies* serves not only as an integral part of the ETO subseries of the United States Army in World War II, but also as a complement and capstone to the portions of The Technical Services subseries that deal with the wartime activities of each of these services in ETO.

Key topics:

1. Theater command and organization, with particular reference to the relationship of tactical and administrative commands (Chs. II, XII, XIII, XIX).

2. The influence of logistical support on the tempo of tactical operations (Chs. I, XIX).

3. Manpower problems, particularly with respect to economy in the use of personnel and in adjustment to unexpected requirements (Chs. XI, XVII).

4. Theater relations with the zone of interior on such matters as organizational policy, supply requirements, and manpower management (Chs. IV, IX, X, XI, XII, XIV, XVII).

5. The use of indigenous resources, both human and material, in the theater of operations (Ch. XVIII).

6. The response to emergencies in military operations, notably with respect to the logistic problems imposed by a reverse (Ch. VI).

7. The accommodation to unusual demands, notably with respect to transportation, as in the case of the final offensive (Ch. XV).

8. The control and allocation of supplies in critically short supply (Chs. IX, XVI).

9. The effect of changes in the scheduled buildup of forces on the prospect of logistic support (Ch. X).

10. The influence of personalities on the working of a theater command and organizational structure (Chs. XII, XIX).

# The Middle East Theater

# The Middle East Theater

This one-volume subseries tells the little-known story of the U.S. Army's mission of assisting the British in their efforts to deliver supplies to the Soviet Union through the Persian Corridor. Initially, the primary American missions involved base construction and the operation of assembly points. This assignment was soon enlarged to include the transportation of materiel to its new ally over a 400-mile network of primitive railroads and highways. From 1942 until the last Soviet soldier left the corridor in 1946, Iran was the silent and little-consulted partner in its destiny, as Britain and the United States struggled to keep the Soviet Union supplied with the military essentials of war. The story thus chronicles the beginnings of an involvement that would culminate in Operation DESERT STORM almost fifty years later.

**THE PERSIAN CORRIDOR AND AID TO RUSSIA.** By *T. H. Vail Motter*. (1952, 1985, 1989; 545 pages, 15 tables, 12 charts, 5 maps, 3 illustrations, glossary, index, CMH Pub 8–1.)

The "Persian Corridor" was one of two major theaters of operations in World War II whose paramount mission was supply. (The other was China-Burma-India.) The Army's mission in Iran was to accelerate the delivery of lend-lease supplies to the Soviet Union. The operation involved delicate and complex relations with three cooperating powers: Great Britain, the USSR, and Iran. These relations transcended logistics and military administration and entered the diplomatic sphere. This volume was written with an awareness of this difficult experiment in cooperation. It is therefore a book for the statesman, administrator, and historian, as well as for officers responsible for future planning in the realm of logistics and strategy. More specifically the book is indispensable to the study of Anglo-American aid to the USSR after the breakdown of the Murmansk route in 1942 and the Anglo-American invasion of North Africa.

The point of view is that of top command responsibility; but all aspects of planning and operations from Washington and London to the "theater" itself are illustrated. The study emphasizes organization and administration as well as achievement in terms of operational results.

In addition to the task of moving supplies through Iran to the Soviet Union, the Army was charged with responsibility for rendering economic and military aid to Iran. This was accomplished by advisory missions to the Iranian Army and the Iranian Gendarmerie (Chs. IX and XXI) and by the broadening of the commander's directive to include economic assistance to Iran (Ch. XX). The volume therefore describes precedents of importance to readers interested in the development of the policy of containment and military assistance, adopted by the United States in the post–World War II era.

Key topics:

1. The use of civilian contractors versus militarization of a large effort of supply in wartime (Chs. II, III, V, VI, VII).

2. Procurement of materiel and manpower (American and Iranian) for construction and the operation of theater services (Chs. VI, VII, XII).

3. Changes in organization required by changes in Allied policy and theater mission (Ch. XI).

4. The problem of overlapping functions and the rivalries between military and civilian (Army, State Department, War Shipping Administration, and Lend-Lease Administration) agencies in an overseas area (Chs. II, IV, XVI–XVIII).

5. Anglo-American command relationships in Iran (Ch. V).

6. Difficulties of cooperation with the USSR (Ch. I).

7. Rivalries between Great Britain and the Soviet Union in Iran and their continued efforts to exclude each other from their respective zones (Chs. VII, XIII).

8. Anglo-American-Soviet negotiations directed toward legalization of the status of American troops in Iran and the relation of these to the Declaration of the Three Powers regarding Iran, 1 December 1943 (Ch. XX).

9. Anglo-American-Iranian negotiations regarding payment for the use of the Iranian State Railway (Ch. XVII).

10. Diplomatic background of the U.S. advisory missions to Iran (Chs. V, XX).

11. Employment of native labor (see Index: "Native employees").

12. Security arrangements in tribal areas (Chs. II, III, V, XI).

13. Planning for expansion of the oil pipeline net in Iran and of the refinery capacity at Bahrein and Abadan (Ch. XV).

14. The role of the Army Service Forces in organizing and administering a supply theater (Ch. X).

15. Command relations between the Middle East Theater and the administration of the Army's responsibilities in Iran (see Index: "U.S. Army Forces in the Middle East (USAFIME); U.S. Military Iranian Mission; U.S. Military North African Mission; Persian Gulf Command; Maxwell, Maj. Gen. Russell L.; Connolly, Maj. Gen. Donald H.; and Shingler, Brig. Gen. Don G.").

16. Shipping—the conflict between global and local interests (see Index: "Shipping").

17. The tendency to overexpand staff and organize beyond the demands of function (Chs. II, III, V, XI).

# The China-Burma-India
# Theater

# The China-Burma-India Theater

The first two volumes of this subseries focus on Lt. Gen. Joseph W. Stilwell, and the third treats his successor, Lt. Gen. Albert C. Wedemeyer, in the China-Burma-India (CBI) Theater. All three works, particularly the account of General Wedemeyer's diplomatic measures, focus on the problems of a major military assistance effort. They not only record the most ambitious U.S.-directed aid program completed during World War II, but also are of general interest for the light they shed on the background of our postwar relations with China. They provide a basis for instructive comparisons of General Wedemeyer's and General Stilwell's exercise of diplomatic and command functions, and of their programs and measures for the reform and training of Chinese forces. Finally, these volumes describe the most extensive experiment during World War II in the sustained supply of ground forces by air.

**STILWELL'S MISSION TO CHINA**. By *Charles F. Romanus* and *Riley Sunderland*. (1953, 1984; 441 pages, 6 tables, 8 charts, 7 maps, 19 illustrations, bibliographical note, glossary, index, CMH Pub 9–1.)

This volume and the next in the subseries are centered on the performance of Lt. Gen. Joseph W. Stilwell. Stilwell was chief of staff to Chiang Kai-shek, in Chiang's capacity of commander in chief of China considered as an Allied theater; he administered U.S. lend-lease aid to China; and he commanded the CBI Theater. Chiang put him in charge of his force (three Chinese armies) in Burma during the ill-fated campaign of 1942, and this campaign, insofar as it involved his authority, is therefore described.

The War Department's concept of aid to China was to help the Chinese to help themselves, by military advice, technical assistance, air support, and supplies needed to fill the gaps in the Chinese armory. General Stilwell was also directed to reopen a ground line of communications with China. The present volume describes General Stilwell's efforts to effect a working relationship with the Generalissimo, to formulate a program acceptable both to the host government and his own superiors, and to organize a logistical base for American assistance and air operations. It presents, in global perspective, the difficulties that were created when the President, overruling the War Department, decided that China-based and air-supplied air power was a better investment of available American resources than rebuilding the Chinese Army.

As theater commander General Stilwell had under his authority a far-flung

Services of Supply (SOS), the Fourteenth Air Force (Maj. Gen. Claire L. Chennault's) in China, and the Tenth Air Force in India. This and the succeeding volumes supplement the more detailed account of these air forces to be found in *The Army Air Forces in World War II*. They are here presented in relation to the missions and activities of the theater and General Stilwell's other responsibilities. This work and its successors also contain a general account of the extraordinary problems and activities of the SOS, plus air supply over the famous "Hump." Their presentation here can be supplemented by consulting the Air Forces history cited and the histories of the technical services in the United States Army in World War II. The present volume covers the period September 1939–September 1943. (The key topics are included in the list that follows the description of the third volume of this subseries.)

**STILWELL'S COMMAND PROBLEMS**. By *Charles F. Romanus* and *Riley Sunderland*. (1955, 1985; 518 pages, 8 charts, 5 tables, 21 maps, 45 illustrations, bibliographical note, glossary, index, CMH Pub 9–2.)

This volume continues the CBI story from October 1943 through General Stilwell's dramatic recall in October 1944. In 1943 the President, overruling the War Department, decided that China-based air power, supplied by air over "the Hump," was a better investment in aid to China than General Stilwell's plans for strengthening, reforming, and employing Chiang Kai-shek's armies, and General Stilwell therefore decided in October 1943 to concentrate his efforts on the India-Burma scene. But his "command problems," already extraordinary, were further complicated by his designation as Deputy Commander, under Lord Mountbatten, of the Southeast Asia Command, and by his responsibility for providing logistical support to the B–29s based in China, as well as to General Chennault's Fourteenth Air Force. During this period the project that was most demanding on General Stilwell's attention finally got under way—the campaign in north Burma to gain control of Myitkyina, to clear the route for the Ledo Road and a pipeline to China, and, in cooperation with the British, to unhinge the Japanese defense of Burma.

The authors sketch the strategic background of this controversial campaign and the Anglo-American debates over it at the Cairo Conference and later. (See also *Strategic Planning for Coalition Warfare: 1943–1944*.) They then describe the campaign in north Burma, with detailed attention to the exhausting thrust of Merrill's Marauders, the major U.S. ground combat force in the theater, to Myitkyina and the long struggle to occupy and hold the town.

In the summer of 1944 Stilwell had once more to give his full attention to China, when the Japanese launched a large-scale offensive and Chiang's forces were unable to prevent them from overrunning Chennault's airfields. Stilwell's proposal, supported by the President, was to put Stilwell in command of the threatened Chinese forces, including some Chinese Communist units that were fighting the Japanese. When Chiang refused to accept Stilwell, the President recalled him. The volume concludes with a well-documented account of these dramatic events, including the mission of General Hurley to China as the President's representative.

**TIME RUNS OUT IN CBI.** By *Charles F. Romanus* and *Riley Sunderland.* (1959, 1985; 428 pages, 7 tables, 5 charts, 15 maps, 76 illustrations, bibliographical note, glossary, index, CMH Pub 9–3.)

*Time Runs Out in CBI* is a history of the two U.S. theaters into which China-Burma-India was split when Stilwell was recalled, one (India-Burma) commanded by Lt. Gen. Daniel I. Sultan, the other (China) by Lt. Gen. Albert C. Wedemeyer. This volume continues and completes the story of the north Burma campaign, recounts the operations of Chinese-American forces along the Salween River, and describes the logistical efforts of General Sultan's command.

The story of General Wedemeyer's attempt to provide the Chinese with an army that they could support and also powerful enough to guarantee China's freedom is the core of this book. By the end of July 1945 Wedemeyer had given thirteen weeks' training to eleven Chinese Nationalist divisions and had started twenty-two more on their first training cycle. To this total, five battle-tested divisions fresh from the Burma campaign could be added. The beginnings of a Chinese Services of Supply to support these 30-odd divisions were at hand, and service schools were functioning. But before this force could advance to the coast, Japan surrendered and time ran out in CBI. The book ends with the Japanese surrender.

Key topics:

1. Strategy (planning) (I, Chs. II, V, VII–X; II, Chs. I, II, X; III, Part II).

2. Lend-lease (see indexes of all three volumes).

3. Conducting a theater SOS (I, Chs. II, VI; II, Chs. III, VII; III, Ch. I, and Part II).

4. U.S. policy toward China (I, Chs. I, II, V, IX; II, Ch. II, and Part III; III, Chs. I, XI).

5. Line of communications problems (I, Chs. VI, VIII, IX; II, Ch. VII; III, Chs. VII, X, XI).

6. Command problems—Allied (I, Chs. III, IV, VIII, IX; II, Chs. II, V, VIII, X, XII; III, Chs. I, V, VIII).

7. Volunteer air forces (I, Chs. I–IV).

8. Local procurement by an SOS directed to "live off the land" (I, Ch. VI; II, Ch. VII; III, Part II).

9. Organizing a theater of operations (I, Chs. II, III, V, X; III, Ch. I).

10. Stilwell's programs for China (I, Chs. III, IV, V, VII, IX, X; II, Chs. I, II).

11. Wedemeyer's programs for China (III, Part II).

12. Stilwell's exercise of command and diplomatic functions (I and II); Wedemeyer's exercise (III, Part II).

13. Campaigning in Burma (see indexes of all three volumes).

14. Chinese training centers (see indexes of all three volumes).

15. Engineering problems (see index entries in all three volumes on roads, airfields, and construction).

16. Airlift to China and supply by air in Burma (see indexes to all three volumes).

17. Strategic air operations based on India and China (see indexes to all three volumes).

# The Technical Services

# The Technical Services

There was a time when armies marched on their stomachs, and providing sufficient quantities of food to the troops was the significant factor in determining the success of a campaign. World War II, however, would forever alter this simplistic view of support as the global needs to supply and sustain a modern army in the field became a reality. Technical support in World War II matured as in no other conflict, tying the home front to the battlefront. The introduction of new technologies, such as radar, the proximity fuse, and the atomic bomb were only a small part of the revolution needed to sustain a modern army at war.

The Technical Services subseries, composed of twenty-four volumes, covers seven technical services representing the combat and combat services branches that the Army still recognizes in 1992. In all cases these volumes were written by the technical historian most knowledgeable on the subject in conjunction with the assistance of the Center of Military History.

## THE CHEMICAL WARFARE SERVICE

When the United States entered World War I, the Army had to prepare to use and cope with poisonous gas, which the Germans had introduced as a weapon on the battlefield of Ypres in April 1915. At first the responsibilities of gas warfare were divided among the Medical Department, the Ordnance Department, the Corps of Engineers, and the Signal Corps, with help from the Bureau of Mines, which conducted research on poisonous gases. In June 1918 the War Department created a Chemical Warfare Service to take over these responsibilities and in 1920 gave it the additional mission of developing other devices of chemical warfare such as smoke, incendiaries, and the 4.2-inch mortor. The three volumes on this service cover this little-known subject from an administrative and tactical standpoint during World War II.

## THE CORPS OF ENGINEERS

The four volumes in this technical service record the vast engineering efforts undertaken by the United States to cope with a global war. Besides the huge task of constructing a continental base for war, the Corps of Engineers had to prepare equipment, troops, and units for action around the globe. Though designated a "technical service," the engineers had more troops in Army Ground Forces units than in those of the Army Service Forces. Additionally the engineers had to provide battle equipment, men, and units trained to use it, as well as to make the Army's maps; construct roads, bridges, and railroads; reconstruct wrecked seaports; and build airfields and military bases in every theater of operations in which American forces were engaged.

## THE MEDICAL DEPARTMENT

The organized services of the Medical Department in war come closer to home to the public than those of the other great supporting services of the Army. The medical and surgical treatment that The Surgeon General and his department gave their millions of patients during World War II, a matter of vital instructive interest to the medical profession, is discussed in the detailed clinical volumes published by the Historical Unit of The Surgeon General's Office. The three medical volumes in the United States Army in World War II series instead focus on the care given to those patients along the medical evacuation chain of command, paying additional attention to such areas as preventive medicine, sanitation, combat psychiatry, organization, and the integration of medical plans into the larger operational and tactical activities in every operational theater.

## THE ORDNANCE DEPARTMENT

The three volumes on this technical service cover the interaction of the Ordnance Department with the Army in the field. As such it complements the combat operational histories while providing the reader with an appreciation of the difficulties of supplying a fighting force.

The first volume on this service is a history of the phases of activity which precede procurement, distribution, and maintenance of fighting equipment, namely, organization, training, research, and development. It is, in short, an analysis of the factors that largely determined the quality of weapons supplied to the Army in World War II. Volume II on the Ordnance Department covers the problems of quantity: production, distribution, and upkeep; and Volume III, operations overseas.

## THE QUARTERMASTER CORPS

Four volumes in The Technical Services subseries trace the Quartermaster Corps as it copes with meeting the staggering and unanticipated demands of a global war. Lack of funding in the interwar years ill prepared the corps for the role it would play in the war against Germany and Japan. As final testimony to its success, a Senate committee would report after the war that "the supply of our armed forces in Europe has been a remarkable achievement, involving the delivery across the ocean and over beaches and through demolished ports, and then over a war-torn countryside into France and Germany of tonnages far in excess of anything previously within the conception of man."

## THE SIGNAL CORPS

The first two of the three volumes on this service present the history of the corps chronologically, rather than topically, unlike the others in The Technical Services subseries. The story is carried forward on a broad front. Although the focus is generally the Office of the Chief Signal Officer in Washington, it follows units of the corps into action on the multiplying overseas theaters of operations. The third volume focuses on the revolution in communications that took place during this period.

## THE TRANSPORTATION CORPS

The three volumes on this corps deal with the youngest of the seven technical services. Created in July 1942 to control the factors that go into the movement of men and munitions, Army transportation would in time become one of the controlling factors in the prosecution of the war. The first two volumes deal with transportation in the United States, with the last volume covering overseas land and water operations.

## THE CHEMICAL WARFARE SERVICE: ORGANIZING FOR WAR. By *Leo P. Brophy* and *George J. B. Fisher*. (1959, 1989; 498 pages, 16 tables, 11 charts, 1 map, 32 illustrations, bibliographical note, glossary, index, CMH Pub 10–1.)

The first part of this volume is an administrative history of the Chemical Warfare Service from its inception until 1946, when it became the Chemical Corps. This part covers the experience of World War I, at home and with the American Expeditionary Forces; the trying years from 1920 to 1939 when the new service had to contend with military parsimony and the public opprobrium attached to gas warfare; and then with the greatly expanded functions of the service in World War II.

In that war the Chemical Warfare Service was responsible for training not only its own service troops and specialized combat units for chemical mortar, smoke generator, and chemical air operations, but also for training the whole Army to cope with chemical warfare, and, incidentally, for training civilians for defense against the use of chemicals in case of enemy attack. These training missions are the subject of Part II.

In 1942 the Chief of the Chemical Warfare Service was designated to head a United States Chemical Warfare Committee, which worked out with the British combined policies and plans for chemical warfare—an experience described in Part I, Chapter IV.

Key topics:
1. The status of gas warfare in international treaties (Ch. II).
2. Plans for use of poisonous gases in World War II (Chs. II–IV).
3. Industrial manpower problems in producing chemical weapons (Ch. VII).
4. Civilian-defense preparations and training (Ch. X).
5. Antigas training of Army air and ground units (Ch. XVI).
6. American preparations for gas warfare in World War I (Ch. I).
7. Problems in wartime expansion of production, testing, and storage facilities (Ch. VI).
8. Problems in the production of training and technical manuals (Ch. XI).

9. The training of officer candidates (Ch. XV).

**THE CHEMICAL WARFARE SERVICE: FROM LABORATORY TO FIELD.**
By *Leo P. Brophy*, *Wyndham D. Miles*, and *Rexmond C. Cochrane*. (1959, 1980; 498 pages, 11 tables, 2 charts, 49 illustrations, 2 appendixes, bibliographical note, glossary, index, CMH Pub 10–2.)

This volume describes and evaluates the record of the Chemical Warfare Service in developing, procuring, and issuing munitions of chemical warfare to the Army and Navy from the inception of the service in World War I. In that war, with the assistance of the Bureau of Mines and the National Research Council, the service developed toxic agents and protective equipment and procured them on a large scale, though few of the items produced had reached the troops of the American Expeditionary Forces when the war ended (Chapter I). In the postwar years of military economy the service could keep only a nucleus of scientists at work on the discovery and designing of its munitions (Chapter II). In the field of procurement and distribution its activity, except for planning, was limited almost entirely to gas masks, manufactured at Edgewood Arsenal and stored at the Edgewood depot (Chapter X).

Increased appropriations and rapid expansion came with the semimobilization of 1939–41, when the service built new laboratories, plants, arsenals, proving grounds, and depots, and began to stock chemical munitions (Chapter X), while its scientists watched the development of munitions that were proving useful in Europe (Chapter II).

The service expanded very rapidly after the United States entered the war. At the heart of its special activities was an augmented technical staff, which worked with the assistance of the Office of Scientific Research and Development and other civilian agencies. The mission of the service was extended to include the offensive and defensive aspects of biological warfare, long under discussion, and now recognized as a serious threat (Chapter V). In pursuing its original mission the service searched for more effective war gases (Chapter III), and better means of physical protection against toxic agents (Chapter IV). It also improved the 4.2-inch chemical mortar into an extremely effective high explosive as well as chemical weapon (Chapter VI); developed what were essentially new weapons: flamethrowers (Chapter VII) and incendiaries (Chapter VIII); and provided better screening smokes and smoke generators (Chapter IX).

The service manufactured these munitions in its arsenals and plants and also procured great quantities of them through contracts with private industry. In addition to problems of procurement that it shared with the other technical services, the Chemical Warfare Service had its own, such as those incident to the relatively modest size of its contracts, and the fact that most of its items had not reached an advanced stage of development (Chapters XIII–XV). The service also had peculiar problems of storage and distribution (Chapter XVI) and unusual difficulties in the field of property disposal (Chapter XVII) because of the nature of its munitions.

Key topics:

1. Cooperation between military and civilian scientists in chemical and biological research (Chs. II, V).

2. Preparations for biological warfare (Ch. V).

3. The role of American industry in the procurement of chemical munitions (Chs. XIV, XV).

4. Research and development procedures (Chs. II, III).

5. Procurement planning (Ch. X).

6. The pricing program (Ch. XII).

7. Renegotiation of war contracts (Ch. XII).

8. The Supply Control System (Ch. XIII).

9. Chemical storage and disposal (Chs. XVI, XVII).

**THE CHEMICAL WARFARE SERVICE: CHEMICALS IN COMBAT.** By *Brooks E. Kleber* and *Dale Birdsell*. (1966, 1984, 1990; 697 pages, 8 charts, 7 maps, 46 illustrations, bibliographical note, glossaries, index, CMH Pub 10–3.)

*Chemicals in Combat*, the last of three volumes devoted to the Chemical Warfare Service (CWS) in World War II, covers the overseas story of that technical service. The first six chapters concern planning, organization, and logistics in the major theaters of operations. Most of the remaining chapters describe the development and combat employment of smoke munitions and generators, the 4.2-inch mortar, the portable and mechanized flamethrowers, and incendiary munitions.

An underlying theme pervades this overseas story. The Chemical Warfare Service was organized in World War I as the vehicle for employing gas munitions and for defending against the use of gas by the enemy. It was thought that these would be the principal roles in World War II. But because gas was not used in the Second World War, the CWS men and units had to justify their presence by undertaking non-gas warfare missions. If there were two key words to describe the overseas CWS experience, they would be "preparedness" for the possible introduction of gas warfare and "improvisation" for the effective use of units in the absence of gas warfare. On top of all this the chemical service was operating in an Army that was not enamored with the traditional chemical mission, let alone the possibility of improvisation.

Had the Allied nations known with certainty what the intentions of the Axis powers were with regard to the use of gas warfare, the U.S. investment in time and materiel might not have been undertaken. On the other hand, had the Allies been any less prepared, one only can guess at what effect that a persistent agent might have had on the D-day landing or at Anzio. If the Japanese had not believed their home land vulnerable to gas they might have used mustard agents against the amphibious forces that slowly penetrated their vast defensive perimeter. The author argues that the U.S. preparedness from gas warfare was worth the effort. Like a "fleet in being," it countered a threat that could have been decisive to the Allied cause if gone unchallenged.

Key topics:

1. Origins of the Chemical Warfare Service in World War I (Ch. I).

2. Development of the Chemical Warfare Service between the two world wars (Chs. I, VII, XI).

3. Adapting a theater CWS staff to a nonchemical environment (Ch. II).

4. Evolution of a theater CWS supply system (Ch. IV).

5. Impact of a dynamic chemical officer in the Central Pacific theater (Chs. V, VI).

6. Diversity of duties of the CWS service units (Ch. VII).

7. The development of the large area smoke installation to conceal ports, beachheads, and river crossings (Chs. VIII, XI).

8. War Department bureaucracy and recalcitrance as illustrated in its reluctance to authorize the 4.2-inch mortar to fire high explosives (Ch. XI).

9. Demand for portable and mechanized flamethrowers in the Pacific theaters (Chs. XIV, XV).

10. Why gas was not used during World War II (Ch. XVIII).

**THE CORPS OF ENGINEERS: TROOPS AND EQUIPMENT**. By *Blanche D. Coll, Jean E. Keith,* and *Herbert H. Rosenthal.* (1958, 1974; 622 pages, 15 tables, 11 charts, 76 illustrations, bibliographical note, glossary, index, CMH Pub 10–4.)

This volume is a history of the measures taken in the United States to cope with the variety of demands placed on the Corps of Engineers during World War II. In the period before Pearl Harbor the dominant theme was preparation to fight in the war of movement that air and armor had introduced on the battlefields of Europe. In the midst of rapid expansion, the corps adopted and procured such equipment as emergency bridges designed to sustain heavier loads, airplane landing mats to take the place of paved runways, powerful earth-moving machinery, and delicate mapping instruments to exploit the possibilities of aerial photography. Such equipment, while greatly increasing the engineer capabilities, also increased its dependence on skilled manpower and on a steady supply of industrial products.

Once the United States was in the war the corps faced global demands not only for more troops, but also for new types of units to reconstruct damaged ports, operate small craft in amphibious landings, distribute petroleum products, manufacture and distribute parts of complicated machinery, and many other incidental tasks. The unexpected lack of skills and aptitudes of a great number of the recruits, the need for hasty training, and the priorities of procurement assigned to weapons immediately required gravely handicapped the engineers. The second part of this work, devoted to 1942, gives an account of the basic decisions and measures adopted to meet the stresses and changes of incessant crises and explores the debate between the corps and the higher echelons of the War Department in the search for realistic compromises.

After 1942, training programs, lengthened and improved in the light of experience, began to produce a more versatile engineer-soldier. Thereafter, too, procurement could be based on more accurately estimated long-range requirements and freer access to materials. The last part of the volume is devoted to this period in which the corps reached its full strength and capacity and in which the orderly distribution of equipment and replacement parts became the primary goal of the corps' logistical activity in the United States.

The whole volume particularizes, and merges into, the comprehensive pictures of mobilization, training, procurement, and supply presented in the Army Ground

Forces volumes on the organization and training of ground combat troops: R. Elberton Smith's *The Army and Economic Mobilization* and Leighton and Coakley's volumes on *Global Logistics and Strategy*.

Key topics:

1. Recruiting and training programs and devices to obtain enough recruits with adequate skills and aptitudes (Chs. V, VII, X–XVIII).

2. Devices to economize manpower, including the development of general-purpose units, in the face of a trend toward specialized types (Chs. I, VI, X, XV).

3. Employment of black troops (Chs. V, VI, X–XI, XIII–XIV).

4. Standardization of equipment (Chs. IX, XXII).

5. Competition between strictly military items and commercial components for industrial facilities (Chs. IV, VIII, IX, XXI).

6. Cooperation with other services and with Allies in the development of equipment (Chs. II, XX).

7. Procedures for allocating supplies among Allies (Chs. VIII, IX).

8. Engineer personnel and training in a period of quasi-mobilization (Ch. V).

9. Organization and functions of engineer troop units (Chs. I–II, VI, X).

10. Organization, functions, equipment, and training of amphibian brigades (Ch. XVI), port reconstruction and repair groups (Ch. XVII), and petroleum distribution companies (Ch. XVIII).

11. Development of engineer equipment (Chs. II, XX).

12. Map supply and strategic intelligence and the division of responsibility among the Corps of Engineers, the Army Air Forces, and nonmilitary agencies in the preparation and supply of maps (Chs. III, XIX).

13. Camouflage (Ch. III).

14. Procurement and distribution of supplies, including the computation of requirements and aid to Allies (Chs. IV, VIII, IX, XXI, XXII).

15. Methods of estimating quantities of supplies needed for construction operations, that is, Class IV requirements (Ch. XXI).

16. Maintenance and the supply of spare parts (Chs. IX, XXII).

17. Procurement and schooling of engineer officers (Chs. V, VII).

18. Replacement training (Chs. VII, XI).

19. Unit training (engineer) under Army Ground Forces, Army Air Forces, and Army Service Forces control (Chs. XII–XV).

**THE CORPS OF ENGINEERS: CONSTRUCTION IN THE UNITED STATES.** By *Lenore Fine* and *Jesse A. Remington*. (1972, 1989; 747 pages, 20 tables, 27 charts, 5 maps, 98 illustrations, appendix, bibliographical note, glossary, index, CMH Pub 10–5.)

Shortly before the United States entered World War II on the side of the Allies, the responsibility for military construction in the United States was transferred from the Quartermaster Corps to the Corps of Engineers. This major shift in mission took place in two steps. First the engineers took charge of Air Corps construction in November 1940. Then, just weeks before the attack on Pearl Harbor, they took over all military construction in support of the expanding Army. In the course of the war, the engineers carried out a multibillion-dollar program of construction. To do this, they converted their decentralized network of field offices from water resource projects to the new mission. The result was a massive engineer construction effort that ranged from the barracks, hospitals, and other buildings that made up entire new camps to munitions factories and the complex and far-flung facilities employed in the Manhattan Project for production of the atomic bomb.

*Construction in the United States* is replete with citations, statistics, and Army organization charts to make clearer an otherwise potentially confusing subject. More importantly this volume is also a history of people: of military leaders and their staffs and of civilian engineers, contractors, and suppliers, giving human interest to the narrative that covers all phases of this remarkable program. After describing the arrangements under which military construction was carried out during World War I and the interwar years, the study covers the political negotiations involved in the change and the many administrative adjustments made by the Corps of Engineers as it adapted to being the Army's construction agent. The authors trace the execution of the mission through the dramatic rapid expansion in 1942 to peak production in 1943. They also cover planning for demobilization, which began during the period of the greatest construction activity.

Key topics:

1. Wartime contracting policies and practices (Chs. I, II, III, V, VIII, XIII, XVII).

2. The use of standardized construction plans (Chs. II, IV, V, X, XVI).

3. Acquisition, control, and apportionment of strategic materials (Chs. II, VI, IX, XVI).

4. Relations between the government, contractors, and labor unions in the construction trades (Chs. V, X).

5. Striking a balance between construction for troops and for industrial production (Chs. VIII–X).

6. Real estate acquisition and disposal (Chs. V, XII, XV).

7. Planning for demobilization (Ch. XVIII).

8. The special characteristics of airfield construction (Chs. XIV, XIX).

9. Construction in support of the Manhattan Project (Ch. XX).

**THE CORPS OF ENGINEERS: THE WAR AGAINST JAPAN.** By *Karl C. Dod.* (1966, 1982; 759 pages, 1 chart, 33 maps, 54 illustrations, 2 appendixes, bibliographical note, glossaries, index, CMH Pub 10–6.)

A companion to the operational volumes in the Army's Pacific theater subseries, this volume chronicles the story of the U.S. Army Corps of Engineers in the most primitive, undeveloped, and remote areas of the Pacific Ocean, China, and Southeast Asia. More often than not, these regions were covered with impenetrable jungles, alive with tropical insects and debilitating diseases, cut by swift and wide rivers, crisscrossed with rugged mountains, and at the end of tenuous supply lines that stretched hundreds, if not thousands, of miles back to developed bases.

Whether in the tropical jungles of Papua–New Guinea or the Burma-China borderlands, on the coral atolls of the Central Pacific, or on the inhospitable islands of the Aleutians, American forces were initially confronted with a lack of even the most rudimentary logistical facilities and with few of the supplies they needed to sustain modern combat operations. They first had to carve out toeholds for bases that could then be tied into the worldwide logistical network that would pump in the men and materiel to press the fight against the Japanese. That difficult job belonged to the Army engineers, who first fought as combat engineers on the front lines and then became the builders who transformed jungles or atolls into new links in the chain of the advanced airfields, ports, and supply bases that would sustain the next forward steps on the road to Tokyo.

The Corps of Engineers began its war against Japan well before the attack on Pearl Harbor as engineer units in Alaska, Hawaii, the Philippine Islands, and Panama labored to improve the defenses of the United States and its vital overseas possessions against hostile attack. After the war began, engineers in the Philippines were consumed in the desperate and unsuccessful campaign to hold Bataan and Corregidor until help arrived. Meanwhile engineer units began flowing into Australia and on to Papua where they developed the bases from which the Allies would begin their long campaign to return to the Philippines.

General MacArthur's strategy of "leapfrogging" up Papua–New Guinea and back to the Philippines stressed avoiding strong Japanese concentrations and seizing and then developing the airfields and bases that would permit his air forces to cover his next leap forward. The success of this approach depended heavily on the ability of his engineer forces to build sufficient facilities quickly under enemy fire, in hostile and primitive conditions, and often with limited supplies of materials and heavy equipment.

Among the most notable of the many achievements of the Army engineers in the Southwest Pacific Area were the operations of the 2d, 3d, and 4th Engineer Special Brigades which conducted all of MacArthur's amphibious assault landings from 1943 through the end of the war. Created in 1942 to conduct the Army's assault landings, the boat and shore operations of the engineer special brigades found their fullest use in MacArthur's numerous amphibious operations.

In the China-Burma-India (CBI) Theater from 1942 through 1944, engineers concentrated on establishing the airfields, supply lines, and bases necessary to sustain British, Indian, Chinese, and American forces facing the Japanese. While many engineer units supported the aerial supply route across the Himalayas (the Hump) and built airfields in China from which U.S. and Chinese air forces struck back at the Japanese and their homeland, others confronted a virtually impassable barrier of mountains, rivers, and jungles in their mission to reestablish an overland supply route to China. By February 1945 Army engineers had driven the Ledo Road and its accompanying petroleum pipeline across the mountains and jungles of northern Burma to link up with the old Burma Road and thus once again opened a secure land route to China for military supplies.

Key topics:

1.  Organization and employment of engineer combat and construction units in support of theater operations (Chs. IV–XV).

2.  The role of engineer units in the Philippine Islands Campaign of 1941–42 (Ch. III).

3.  The role of combat engineers in combined arms operations (Chs. III–VI, X–XV).

4.  Planning and conduct of amphibious landing operations by engineer special brigades (Chs. VI, XIII–XIV).

5.  The development of bases and lines of communications in remote and undeveloped areas (Chs. IV, VII, X–XV).

6.  Airfield and air base development in primitive areas (Chs. IV–VI, X–XV).

7.  Employment of black engineer units (Chs. IV–VII, XIV–XV).

8.  The effect of modern construction equipment and mechanization on engineer operations (Chs. IV–XV).

9.  The prewar strengthening of defenses in Panama, Hawaii, and Alaska (Chs. I–II).

10. Interrelationship of strategy, logistics, and construction (Chs. IV–V, IX–XV).

**THE CORPS OF ENGINEERS: THE WAR AGAINST GERMANY**. By *Alfred M. Beck, Abe Bortz, Charles W. Lynch, Lida Mayo*, and *Ralph F. Weld.* (1985; 608 pages, 5 charts, 30 maps, 88 illustrations, bibliographical note, glossary, index, CMH Pub 10–22.)

This volume parallels the preceding one, treating the Army Corps of Engineers in the Mediterranean and European theaters. There Army engineers were called upon to provide their traditional combat missions in offensive and defensive ground operations as well as the construction support needed to develop the logistical structure to sustain those operations. But the requirements of modern war against powerful foes demanded that they played new and innovative roles, such as in amphibious operations, airfield development for tactical and strategic air forces, aerial photography and mapping, and port reconstruction and repair.

While constructing the support and training base for American forces in the United Kingdom, U.S. Army engineers were severely tested during combat operations in North Africa, Sicily, and Italy. New tactical bridging equipment, such as the Bailey and treadway bridges, were successfully employed as were new heavy construction equipment, such as Caterpillar tractors and LeTourneau scrapers, which provided American engineers with a significant advantage over their opposing counterparts. First encountered in Tunisia, the German adeptness at mine warfare was a serious challenge which the combat engineers never completely overcame through the remainder of the war. In this area, as in others, technology could not replace the human skills of the individual engineer.

This volume records the slow and methodical operations of the Italian campaign which placed a high premium on the more traditional skills of the combat engineer —laying and clearing minefields, building and assaulting field fortifications, and developing and maintaining supply lines. Siege operations against a dug-in enemy in mountainous terrain, in which engineers played a critical role, replaced mobile warfare for months on end. In such operations, base development and the buildup of supplies were of importance to each forward leap and often determined the actual timing for each movement.

During the Normandy Campaign of 1944, Army engineer efforts supported the initial lodgment and then the ensuing war of movement: clearing mines, conducting assault river crossings, erecting temporary tactical bridges, and rebuilding roads, airfields, and railways. Bridging, in fact, proved critical to the war in northern Europe due to the many rivers, canals, and lesser water courses that characterized the terrain. Allied progress often depended on the rapidity with which engineers could repair existing highway and rail spans, construct new ones, and replace critical assault bridging with more permanent structures.

Also treated are engineers efforts to assist the military government in restoring basic services throughout liberated western Europe and newly occupied Germany and to build and maintain the logistical infrastructure that supported the permanent American forces stationed there.

Key topics:

1. Role of engineers in the United Kingdom, 1942 (Ch. III).

2. Preparation and conduct of amphibious operations by engineer units (Chs. IV, VI, VII, XIV, XV, XVI, XXIII).

3. Siege operations in Europe (Chs. XVII, XIX).

4. Petroleum, oil, and lubricant operations and doctrine (Chs. V, XI, XIII, XX).

5. Organization of engineer units (Chs. II, IV, XIV, XVIII).

6. Mine warfare in Tunisia and Europe (Chs. V, IX, X, XIV, XVII).

7. Preparation, planning, and conduct for D-day (Chs. XIII–XVI).

## THE MEDICAL DEPARTMENT: HOSPITALIZATION AND EVACUATION, ZONE OF INTERIOR. By *Clarence McKittrick Smith*. (1956, 1983, 1989; 503 pages, 18 tables, 16 charts, 28 illustrations, bibliographical note, glossary, index, CMH Pub 10–7.)

The Surgeon General in World War II was responsible for designing, building, equipping, and operating the Army's great system of hospitals in the United States and for the movement to them of patients from overseas and in the zone of interior. His department was also the matrix and forge of the hospitals and evacuation units sent to theaters of operations throughout the world, and it selected, trained, and equipped them. Planning and improvement of methods to meet these complex responsibilities constitute the main theme of the present volume.

The author's well-documented exposition of this theme focuses on large-scale hospital administration, to include medical construction, training, procurement, logistics, and command organization. Included are treatments of The Surgeon General's sometime difficult relationships with the Quartermaster General, the Chief of Engineers, the Chief of Transportation, and the Commanding Generals of the Army Air Forces and the Army Service Forces in matters of responsibility and jurisdiction.

Key topics:

1. The resolution of problems of authority and responsibility with other authorities concerned with hospitalization and evacuation (Chs. I, IV, IX).

2. Forecasting bed requirements and planning new construction to meet them (Chs. II, III, V, XI, XII, XVII).

3. Development of new types of hospitals and evacuation units for theaters of operations (Chs. VI, VIII, X, XVI, XXV).

4. Simplification of administrative procedures and internal organization of hospitals (Chs. VII, XIII, XIV, XV).

5. Redesigning of vehicles for moving patients (Chs. XXII, XXIII, XXIV).

6. Forecasting the number of patients to be evacuated from overseas (Ch. XIX).

7. Creation of a unified system for distributing patients among hospitals in the United States (Chs. XX, XXI).

**THE MEDICAL DEPARTMENT: MEDICAL SERVICE IN THE MEDITERRANEAN AND MINOR THEATERS**. By *Charles M. Wiltse*. (1965, 1978, 1989; 664 pages, 39 tables, 43 maps, 128 illustrations, 4 appendixes, bibliographical note, glossary, index, CMH Pub 10–8.)

*The Medical Department: Medical Service in the Mediterranean and Minor Theaters* is the first of three volumes concerning the administrative history of the Army Medical Department's overseas operations in World War II. The initial chapter covers the work of the Army Medical Department at the Atlantic outposts established in 1941 before the initiation of major deployments to the Mediterranean and European theaters. The remaining chapters describe the Army medical service in the campaigns in North Africa, Sicily, Italy, and southern France. Included in the appendixes are a survey of the organization and operations of the German medical service and a brief discussion of the hospitalization and evacuation system of French forces serving with U.S. troops in the theater.

In the Mediterranean theater, where U.S. Army troops launched their first ground offensive in the fall of 1942, the organization, equipment, and techniques of the Medical Department were tested under a wide variety of conditions from the deserts of North Africa to the mountains and marshes of Italy. The experience acquired significantly benefited later campaigns in both Europe and the Pacific. Of particular importance is the pioneering work on combat psychiatry which was begun on an experimental basis in Tunisia and Sicily.

From 1944, when the campaign in northern Europe first began siphoning veteran medical formations and their facilities from Italy, to the spring of 1945, when the Germans surrendered, untried replacements and chronic shortages of equipment and supplies handicapped the medical service in the Mediterranean theater. The work documents the ingenuity and skill required by medical officers to prevent disease and to provide evacuation, hospitalization, and care for the sick and wounded in a theater that had become a secondary effort. Finally, the study covers the activities of Army medical personnel who remained in southern Europe supporting the occupation force

and the local governments, until the last U.S. forces left Italy in December 1947.
    Key topics:
    1. Preventive medicine in a tropical climate (Chs. I–II, V, XV).
    2. Public health in the aftermath of war (Chs. II, V, XI, XIII).
    3. Medical support of widely dispersed troop concentrations (Chs. I–II).
    4. Medical support of major amphibious operations (Chs. III, IV, VI–VII, X, XV).
    5. Preventive medicine and insect-borne disease (Chs. I, II, IV, VI, VII–X, XV).
    6. Combat psychiatry (Chs. III, IV, VI–XI, XIII, XV).
    7. Prevention and treatment of venereal disease (Chs. I, II, VI, VIII–X).
    8. Training of medical troops (Ch. IV).
    9. Air evacuation (Chs. I–V, VII, VIII, X, XI, XIII, XIV).
    10. Medical care and hospitalization of prisoners of war (Chs. V, IX, XII, XIV).

**THE MEDICAL DEPARTMENT: MEDICAL SERVICE IN THE EURO-
PEAN THEATER OF OPERATIONS**. By *Graham A. Cosmas* and *Albert E.
Cowdrey*. (1992; 652 pages, 9 tables, 12 charts, 6 diagrams, 27 maps, 102
illustrations, bibliographical note, glossary, index, CMH Pub 10–23.)

    This volume tells the story of the U.S. Army medical service in the largest
American land campaign of World War II. Primarily an operational and logistical
rather than a clinical history, it follows the development of the theater medical service
from the beginning of the U.S. Army buildup in Great Britain early in 1942 through
the Normandy invasion, the advance across France and the Low Countries, and the
overrunning of the Third Reich.
    The European theater Chief Surgeon, Maj. Gen. Paul R. Hawley, and his
assistants assembled and trained over a quarter million medical personnel; established
hospitals containing hundreds of thousands of beds in Great Britain and on the
Continent; solved problems of supply; safeguarded troop health; and developed a
complex system of air, sea, rail, and ambulance evacuation. In occupied Germany,
they encountered and overcame a situation new to American armies: the surrender and
imprisonment of a whole enemy army, numbering in the millions; the liberation of
other millions of prisoners and displaced persons; and the care of a conquered people
who were both industrialized and highly urbanized. In the process, the medical
service met the challenges of working with Allies, supporting fast-moving mechanized forces, adapting units and equipment for unanticipated missions, and integrat-
ing the latest findings of medical science into a comprehensive system of patient care.
This is, however, more than a story of high policy. Also described are the efforts and
achievements of frontline aidmen, litterbearers, and ambulance drivers; doctors and
nurses in hospitals; and the thousands of other American medical soldiers. Often
unsung, usually overworked, and occasionally in mortal danger, they gave effect to
abstract plans through countless acts of courage and compassion.
    This account chronicles theater medical planning and operations under conditions
of modern, high-intensity combat. It also constitutes a case study in the workings of
combat service support in wartime and illustrates principles of medical organization
that remain timeless. Finally, this account dramatically reaffirms the truth that Army

medicine requires for success in war doctors who are also soldiers, who understand the workings of the other branches of service, and who are able to cooperate effectively with them.

Key topics:

1. The solution of problems of command and control of the medical service and its relations with other combat and support elements (Chs. I, II, III, XIII, XVI, XVII).

2. Forecasting hospital bed requirements and planning and executing new construction to meet them (Chs. I, II, IV, VIII, X, XIV, XVII).

3. Improvisation of new types of hospitals and evacuation units within a theater of operations (Chs. V, VII, IX, X, XI).

4. Operations of field army, corps, and division medical service in a variety of tactical situations (Chs. VI, VII, IX, XI, XII, XV).

5. Procurement and training of medical personnel and medical units in a theater of operations (Chs. II, V, XIII, XVII).

6. Integration of medical and operational planning (Chs. I, II, VI, IX).

7. Theater and field army medical supply (Chs. II, VI, VII, IX, X, XI, XIII, XVII).

8. Development of a theater evacuation policy and evacuation system (Chs. IV, VIII, X, XIV, XVII).

9. Preventive medicine in garrison and during combat operations (Chs. I, V, VII, XIV, XV, XVI, XVII).

10. The medical role in civil affairs and disaster relief in the aftermath of war (Chs. XVI, XVII).

**THE MEDICAL DEPARTMENT: MEDICAL SERVICE IN THE WAR AGAINST JAPAN.** By *Mary Ellen Condon-Rall* and *Albert E. Cowdrey.* (CMH Pub 10–24, forthcoming.)

This volume treats the medical history of the war against Japan, a story that was as varied as the theater itself, which covered approximately a third of the surface of the earth. The South and Southwest Pacific Areas and the China-Burma-India Theater were ravaged by tropical diseases; cold injury was a problem in the Aleutian fighting; and combat surgery was everywhere important. The need to fight a war on islands required the Army to make many changes in a force structure designed for land combat, and the Medical Department followed suit in order to provide medical support on the beaches, during the move inland, and in deep jungle fighting beyond the reach of vehicles.

Command arrangements differed as widely as the physical environment. Theater surgeons were obliged to work in both Army- and Navy-run theaters and within joint and combined command structures. The complications that resulted, especially in the Southwest Pacific Area, were significant not only because coherent medical policy was long delayed, but because of the special difficulties of the Pacific war. Command support was needed to assign medical materiel the high priorities that it needed in order to cross thousands of miles of open ocean and arrive at the proper location, at the right time, and in adequate quantity. Even more important, command support was absolutely essential to enforce the rules of preventive medicine so vital to troop health while fighting in primitive and highly malarial lands.

In the South and Southwest Pacific the authors record the complex medical learning process that took place. Although troops in both theaters had been in combat from the first days of the war, their lack of time for preparation was reflected in the early epidemics that weakened both the defenders of Bataan and the conquerors of Guadalcanal and Papua. Hard-won mastery of preventive medicine and amphibious medical organization contributed crucially to the later triumphs of American arms. In all the Pacific theaters, amphibious medical support was a complex art that was learned and perfected to a great extent under enemy fire. In the Central Pacific Area the treatment and evacuation of wounded rather than fighting disease became the centerpiece of medical activity. Finally, medical personnel in the China-Burma-India Theater devoted their efforts not only to support of the small American forces, but to aiding the miserably ill-equipped Chinese armies and teaching the rudiments of medicine to young Chinese officers.

Although care of American and Allied forces grew ever more sophisticated, medical support for guerrillas and prisoners of war continued to be primitive in many respects. Care of civilians injured in the fighting gradually improved, however, leading to the successful efforts of the postwar military government in Japan to suppress disease among former enemies, preserve life, and provide for the victims of the atomic bombs.

Key topics:

1. The organization of a theater medical service in joint and combined commands (Chs. II, III, VII, XI, XIII).

2. Medical interaction with Allied civil health authorities in wartime (Chs. II, VII, X, XII).

3. The organization of medical support for operations in primitive regions (Chs. IV, VI, IX).

4. Medical support of amphibious operations (Chs. IV, V, VI, X).

5. Medical support of guerrilla bands (Ch. XI).

6. The provision of medical care for conquered populations (Ch. XIII).

7. Medical consequences of a nuclear attack (Ch. XIII).

**THE ORDNANCE DEPARTMENT: PLANNING MUNITIONS FOR WAR.** By *Constance McLaughlin Green, Harry C. Thomson,* and *Peter C. Roots.* (1955, 1970, 1990; 542 pages, 14 tables, 18 charts, 54 illustrations, bibliographical note, glossary, index, CMH Pub 10–9.)

This first volume includes background material, reaching from the early nineteenth century to the outbreak of war in Europe in 1939 (Chs. I–III). The research and development programs, 1919 to 1939, receive special attention because of their direct effect upon much of the later work. The main emphasis of the book nevertheless falls upon the period 1939 to 1945.

While endeavoring to examine dispassionately the attitudes of other agencies within and outside the Army, the authors present the story chiefly from the point of view of the Ordnance Department. Chapter III gives a brief account of the financing of the department's activities before and during World War II in order to put the discussion of policies and procedures, accomplishments and failures, into a meaningful setting. It includes a rapid survey of the consequences of lend-lease, supplemental to the data in *Global Logistics and Strategy*. Chapter IV highlights the framework within which the department worked, the organization created by the two wartime Chiefs of Ordnance, and the revisions demanded by Army reorganization and the appearance of new civilian agencies; it also explains not only the major organizational features but also the philosophy underlying them and the sources of conflict between the Ordnance Department and other agencies. Two subsequent chapters (V and VI) cover recruitment and training of personnel to carry on the expanded tasks of the department. The rest of the volume deals with research and development problems.

Much of the section on research and development contains a discussion of particular items developed to meet particular military needs. It focuses therefore on the problem of translating combat requirements into feasible "development requirements" and the steps the Ordnance Department took to satisfy them. Hence the chapters on ordnance for ground warfare (X–XIII) deal with the development of equipment designed to embody all three desiderata of modern warfare: the greatest possible mobility, maximum firepower, and utmost protection for troops. A chapter (XIV) on weapons for ground defense against aerial attack constitutes the bridge between the data on ground and air equipment, while Chapters XV through XVII on aircraft armament analyze the characteristics of adequate airborne weapons and the work of the Ordnance Department in endeavoring to develop suitable airborne guns, rockets, and bombs. Comparisons with German concepts, methods, and results throw added light on much of the American research and development program. Finally, in Chapter XVIII, exploration of the difficulties resulting from the shortage of strategically important raw materials and description of the means devised to conserve them further explain ordnance quandaries.

Key topics:

1. Relations between the Ordnance Department and higher echelons of the War Department, other technical services, and civilian research agencies (Ch. IV, VIII).

2. Decentralization versus centralized control of ordnance activities (Ch. IV).

3. Problems of the ordnance training program (Chs. V, VI).

4. The relationship of doctrine of tactical use to the development of new weapons (Ch. IX).

5. The role of technical intelligence and exchange of scientific data with Allied nations (Chs. VII, IX).

6. The time lag between completion of an experimental weapon and its employment in combat: German and American views on "battle-testing" (Ch. IX).

7. Armor and firepower versus lightness, maneuverability, and numbers: the tank controversy (see Index: "Tanks").

8. For other ordnance items, see index listings for particular types of materiel.

**THE ORDNANCE DEPARTMENT: PROCUREMENT AND SUPPLY.** By *Harry C. Thomson* and *Lida Mayo*. (1960, 1980, 1991; 504 pages, 24 tables, 2 charts, 52 illustrations, bibliographical note, glossary, index, CMH Pub 10–10.)

This volume fits the activities of the Ordnance Department into the larger pictures of procurement and supply to be found in *The Army and Economic Mobilization* and the two volumes on *Global Logistics and Strategy*. The story focuses on the particular items that ordnance officers were tasked to procure and supply: artillery and small arms, and ammunition for both; fire-control instruments; combat vehicles, including the tank; the transport vehicles that put the Army and its supplies on motor-driven wheels; and spare parts and maintenance for all of these. How it provided and maintained such vital instruments of war is of interest to all who depended on them for effectiveness in combat, and not less so to employers and employees in the great American industries, such as the automotive, whose plants and skills the Army drew into its service to aid in producing these instruments.

This volume complements *Planning Munitions for War*, which describes the development of Ordnance Department weapons. The section on procurement in the present volume centers on the department's Industrial Division, the manufacturing arsenals, and the district offices; the section dealing with supply concentrates on the Field Service Division and the depots and changes in the depot system introduced to improve delivery all over the globe of the right kinds of munitions in the right quantities.

At the outset the authors describe the problems of the department in launching the munitions program of 1940 and in the basic task of computing requirements. They examine the need for new construction, both of depot and manufacturing facilities, as a factor in lengthening the gap between the decision to rearm and readiness to deploy adequately armed combat forces. They give full weight to the strong ties developed over the years between the Ordnance Department and industry through the procurement districts, the manufacturing arsenals, and the Army Ordnance Association and describe, in nontechnical language, wartime manufacturing methods and new techniques of production. In a succession of "commodity chapters" the volume explores the most serious problems that the department had to overcome in procuring or producing a class of equipment, such as artillery, tanks, ammunition of various types, and vehicles, repeatedly emphasizing the critical importance of machine tools for the production of fighting equipment. The rest of the volume tells how the department stored and distributed the enormous quantities and varieties of munitions produced and gives particular attention to problems of cataloging and stock control.

Key topics:

1. Requirements and the difficulties attending the establishment of firm, long-range production objectives (Ch. IV).

2. The Ordnance Department's experience with conflicting demands for mass production and for improvements in design (Chs. V–XI).

3. Arsenals: their role as repositories of production knowledge and as centers for overhaul and modification of materiel in storage (Chs. V–IX).

4. Ordnance experience with the problem of spare parts, especially for tanks and trucks (Ch. XIII).

5. Measures to regulate and speed up the movement of ordnance from factory to depot to troops (Chs. XVII, XVIII).

6. Devices, such as standardization of nomenclature and parts numbering

(especially important for spare parts), stock control, and use of electrical accounting machines in reporting depot stocks, to bring about more efficient stockage and distribution of ordnance materiel (Chs. XIX, XX).

7. The creation of ordnance troop units suitable for supply, repair, and preventive maintenance and the problem of working out effective management of maintenance shops in the zone of interior through the service command system set up by the Army Service Forces (Ch. XXII).

**THE ORDNANCE DEPARTMENT: ON BEACHHEAD AND BATTLE-FRONT.** By *Lida Mayo*. (1968, 1978, 1991; 523 pages, 25 tables, 4 charts, 69 illustrations, 8 maps, bibliographical note, glossary, index, CMH Pub 10–11.)

*On Beachhead and Battlefront* tells the evolving story of combat service support for items of ordnance equipment and ammunition. The volume concentrates on the European, Mediterranean, and Southwest Pacific Theaters of Operations, drawing a distinction among these theaters of war and the type of support demanded in each theater of operations. Other areas, such as the China-Burma-India Theater and the South Pacific, Caribbean, and Alaska, are mentioned only in passing or in how they support the main theaters of operations. The author provides rich combat service support contrasts and similarities between Pacific and European theaters. Beginning with the Army's first offensives in Burma, Papua, and North Africa, the narrative then follows the invasion of Europe beginning with Sicily, cumulating in victory in Europe. The story then returns to the Pacific to describe the invasions of New Guinea, the Philippines, and Okinawa. Ordnance support for both operational planning and execution are the central themes.

The author carefully begins each campaign with a brief military geographical overview, discusses the planning and conduct of ensuing operations, and then details the ordnance combat service support that was provided. Planning is first considered and then contrasted with execution. In each of the unfolding campaigns the author details the units and men conducting ordnance support, drawing extensively upon the detailed ordnance records down to unit level to give the reader a sense of the issues that might otherwise be lost.

The volume also details the organizational concept of support, pointing out the various echelons of support in each theater, but focusing on field army level and the support given to subordinate corps and divisions. In each case units, commanders, planners, and soldiers are mentioned with illustrations of their changing combat circumstance, and doctrinal issues of organization, levels of stockage, command, control, and communications are fully portrayed. The evolving ordnance organizational concept of support reflected the changing command and control needs of the various campaigns. The study thus contrasts the mobility and transport requirements for equipment coming into each theater and the demands placed on ordnance support under combat conditions. In each case maintenance support was effected as far forward as feasible.

This volume also evaluates U.S. equipment and compares it to Axis equipment, not only in quality and quantity, but the rapidity with which it was fielded. Further, by detailing each successive campaign, this volume accents the continued improvisation and imagination generated by ordnance personnel. Towed sleds behind tanks in Italy, hedgerow cutting tanks in Normandy, and barge-mounted maintenance shops in the Philippines, all contributed to successful combat service support to the frontline soldier.

Key topics:

1. Ammunition support to the forces in the field (Chs. X, XV, XIX, XXI).

2. Maintenance support in mud, snow, sand, and jungle (Chs. V, XXI, XXIV).

3. Preparation for invasion (Ch. XIII).

4. Importance of early realistic combat assessment of maintenance and ammunition support (Chs. X, XI, XX).

5. Continued need for transportation by truck or water with attendant need for tires and major assemblies (Chs. V, VII, XII).

6. Continual equipment combat evaluation and improvement through improvisation and imaginative replacement by new equipment (Chs. XVII, XXIII).

**THE QUARTERMASTER CORPS: ORGANIZATION, SUPPLY, AND SERVICES, VOLUME I**. By *Erna Risch*. (1953, 1987; 418 pages, 11 charts, 25 illustrations, bibliographical note, glossary, index, CMH Pub 10–12.)

**THE QUARTERMASTER CORPS: ORGANIZATION, SUPPLY, AND SERVICES, VOLUME II**. By *Erna Risch* and *Chester L. Kieffer*. (1955, 1983; 433 pages, 19 tables, 3 charts, 30 illustrations, bibliographical note, glossary, index, CMH Pub 10–13.)

A military force is a separated community, what sociologists call a "segregative community," and in modern war it becomes a huge one. An army (or navy) has not only to forge an effective fighting force out of this vast community and arm it, but also to feed and clothe it, and, in general, step into the place of a thousand private and public enterprises that normally provide for its daily human needs. The principal business of the Quartermaster Corps in World War II was to provide the housing, food, clothes, personal equipment, and fuel for a community that numbered, first and last, between eleven and twelve million men and women. It also provided laundry, bath, and other services. The corps became therefore at once a bridge and a transforming agency between the civilian economy and a "nation in arms" which was soon deployed throughout the globe.

These two volumes show that the Quartermaster Corps was unprepared for this staggering task, partly because of financial starvation, partly from lack of vision and flexibility, largely because of demands that could not be anticipated. Food and clothing, for example, while they had to be standardized for mass procurement, had also to be adapted and varied for use in every diversity of climate and terrain. Equipment had to be reduced in bulk since mobility of force was at a premium and cargo shipping was one of the Allies' scarcest resources throughout the war.

These volumes describe the vigor, ingenuity, and resourcefulness with which the Quartermaster General and his corps attacked a bewildering variety of tasks and emphasize failures as well as successes. Even the most successful expedients were often distasteful to the individual soldier who had to endure dehydrated vegetables and fruits, egg and milk powders, and similar prepackaged edibles. Improvements were often slow. When, for example, GIs refused to use lemon powder except to scrub floors, the Quartermaster Corps simply stopped having it made.

These volumes also detail the cooperation of American industry with the Army on a vast scale. The Quartermaster General engaged over two hundred firms in tasks of research and development and covered a larger sector of the normal civilian economy in procuring supplies needed by the Army than did any other service. Another major story centers around the administration of those supplies. Essentially, the Quartermaster Corps developed a commodity-functional type of organization and stock control system to effect economy and achieve a balanced distribution of supplies. The result is a history of mass organization operating under high pressures, capable of improvisation, and sufficiently flexible to perform its huge task effectively.

Both volumes describe the Quartermaster Corps at work in the zone of interior. Volume I, after treating the reorganization and expansion of the corps at the outbreak of war and sketching its wartime organization (Introduction and Ch. I), deals with research and development (Chs. II–V), procurement and production control (Chs. VI–VIII), storage and warehousing operations (Ch. IX), and stock control (Ch. X). Volume II treats salvage and reclamation (Chs. I–II) and the problems of industrial demobilization (Ch. III), and includes a statistical review (Ch. IV) reflecting the magnitude and proportions of quartermaster operations in World War II. It completes the picture of zone of interior activities with an account of the recruiting, assignment, and training of quartermaster personnel (Chs. V–IX) and of such special services of the corps as the procurement of animals (Ch. X), its operation of laundry and dry-cleaning establishments (Ch. XI), and its provisions for the care of the dead (Ch. XII).

Key topics:

1. Forecasting Army requirements (I, Ch. VI).
2. Requirements and procurement (I, Chs. II, VI).
3. Factors affecting technical military research in preparation for war and in wartime (I, Chs. II–V).
4. Effects of the 1942 reorganization of the War Department on the Quartermaster Corps (I, Ch. I).
5. Streamlining procurement procedures during the war (I, Ch. VII).
6. Expediting production (I, Ch. VIII).
7. Wartime expansion of storage facilities (I, Ch. IX).
8. Development of stock control (I, Ch. X).
9. Conservation of supplies (II, Ch. II).
10. Contract termination (II, Ch. III).
11. Industrial demobilization (II, Ch. III).
12. The Quartermaster General and the Army Service Forces (I, Ch. I).
13. Army clothing development (I, Ch. III).
14. Ration development (I, Ch. V).
15. Packaging and packing of quartermaster supplies (I, Chs. V, IX).
16. Inspection of quartermaster supplies (I, Ch. VIII).

17. Use of material-handling equipment (I, Ch. IX).
18. Mechanizing the handling of equipment (I, Ch. IX).
19. Disposal of surplus property (I, Ch. X; II, Ch. III).
20. Salvage operations (II, Ch. I).
21. Development and training of quartermaster units (II, Ch. IX).
22. Use of dogs in war (II, Ch. X).
23. Operation of Army laundries (II, Ch. XI).
24. Care of the dead (II, Ch. XII).

**THE QUARTERMASTER CORPS: OPERATIONS IN THE WAR AGAINST JAPAN**. By *Alvin P. Stauffer*. (1956, 1978, 1990; 358 pages, 3 maps, 29 illustrations, bibliographical note, glossary, index, CMH Pub 10–14.)

This book is an analytical history of quartermaster activities in three great U.S. theater commands in the war against Japan: the Southwest Pacific, South Pacific, and Central Pacific Areas. Since Army elements were most numerous in General MacArthur's command, the Southwest Pacific is treated at greater length than the others. But the author, observing in general a chronological sequence, has linked the diverse developments in the three commands.

The narrative includes the efforts of quartermasters in 1941 to equip the Philippine Army for a hostile attack, an undertaking largely frustrated by lack of time and the initial American strategy of meeting invasion at the beach line. This strategy called for dispersion of stocks that had been painfully accumulated at depots that were thus soon overrun and had to be destroyed to avert capture. Complementing *The Fall of the Philippines*, the volume then recounts the ingenious efforts on Bataan to stave off starvation by fishing, harvesting local rice crops, and slaughtering carabao and the brave but tragic attempts to break through the strangling Japanese blockade and bring in food from the southern Philippines and from Australia and the Dutch East Indies.

The narrative then focuses on food-importing Hawaii. There the Army, fearing a Japanese invasion, gave the quartermaster of the Hawaiian Department an extraordinary role as controller of civilian food supplies. Hawaii, New Zealand, and Australia were the only land masses in the Pacific that had been sufficiently developed to serve as major bases. Remoteness from the United States and shipping shortages put a premium on local procurement of military necessities in the two British commonwealths, especially Australia, which became major suppliers of subsistence and provided large quantities of other items.

The corps was also confronted with extraordinary difficulties of supply over the long lines running from depots in the United States to widely scattered island bases in territory that lacked the basic facilities for storage and distribution. The author describes how these difficulties were surmounted and troops on tiny atolls and jungleclad islands were supplied, giving close attention to interruptions of supply to bases and troops. The volume includes an evaluation of the utility of the various items of individual and organizational equipment under the exceptional conditions of island and tropical warfare and covers the whole gamut of quartermaster responsibilities in the field, from bakeries, baths, laundry, salvage, and graves registration, to the supply of food and clothing.

Key topics:

1. The influence of logistical unpreparedness on capacity for defense (Luzon) (Ch. I).

2. Logistical planning for island campaigns (Ch. X).

3. Relationship of military command to the civilian population under conditions of martial law (Hawaii) (Ch. II).

4. Overseas supply mission and organization (Chs. II–VI).

5. Problems of local procurement in foreign lands (Ch. V).

6. Operations of island supply bases (Chs. IV, VI, VII, VIII).

7. Supply distribution problems in island warfare (Chs. VI, VII, VIII).

8. Theater relations with the zone of interior in supply matters (Ch. VI).

9. Automatic resupply of combat forces (Ch. VI).

10. Supply under operational conditions (Chs. VI, VIII, X, XI).

11. Evaluation of the provision of personal services and comforts (Ch. IX).

12. Evaluation of items of individual and organizational equipment in tropical combat (Ch. XI).

## THE QUARTERMASTER CORPS: OPERATIONS IN THE WAR AGAINST GERMANY. By *William F. Ross* and *Charles F. Romanus*. (1965, 1979, 1991; 798 pages, 21 tables, 4 charts, 3 maps, 39 illustrations, bibliographical note, glossary, index, CMH Pub 10–15.)

The chief function of the U.S. Army Quartermaster Corps in Europe was to provide food and clothing for the troops. But it was also involved in such work as supplying laundry and bath facilities; collecting, identifying, and burying the dead; providing fuel, shelter, and the liquor ration; supplying spare parts and salvaging useful items; handling captured enemy equipment; and acting as supply custodian to the far-flung civil affairs organization. By the spring of 1945, the Quartermaster Corps in the Mediterranean and European theaters was furnishing necessities and comforts to more than seven and one-half million people, of whom 60 percent were Allies, civilians, and prisoners of war. It was the largest human support operation by a single organization to that time.

This study emphasizes the higher levels of quartermaster activity at different periods of the war against the Axis. In the Mediterranean Theater of Operations encompassing North Africa, Sicily, and Italy, stress has been placed on the roles of the corps, army, and base section quartermasters, while in the European theater greater attention has been given to the problems of the Theater Chief Quartermaster. This difference in approach springs from differences between the two theaters. The Mediterranean theater evolved more slowly, with strong British involvement. In the Mediterranean, moreover, there was greater influence upon operations by junior logistical commanders and staff officers than in the more elaborate and tightly knit theater organization to the north.

Dominating quartermaster activity in the European Theater of Operations was a toweringly energetic soldier—Maj. Gen. Robert M. Littlejohn. His frustrations, mistakes, and triumphs in organizing supply for highly mechanized continental warfare and his efforts to maintain a strong position with respect to G–4 and the other technical services provide the principal narrative thread for this volume. From the moment of his arrival in London in 1942 as a key member of the special staff in the Services of Supply, the history of the quartermaster support mission in Europe is inseparably associated with the officer who headed it.

He touched the cardinal issues of the day: the multifaceted logistical planning effort in England for the great cross-Channel attack; the crisis of "frantic supply" during the race across France in mid-1944; the winter clothing and trench foot controversy during the stalemate a few months later; and the controversy over prisoner-of-war rations amid the theater and worldwide food shortage in 1945. General Littlejohn's last assignment in the European theater was head of the Graves Registration Command, an effort representing the largest item of unfinished quartermaster business in the liberated countries as the fighting came to a close.

Key topics:

1. Forecasting logistical requirements and developing logistical planning factors (Chs. II, V, VI, VII, IX, XI, XV–XVIII).

2. Automatic and standard supply procedures (Chs. IX, XII).

3. Development of a theater troop basis (Chs. II, IV, XI, XII, XIV).

4. Training of logistical forces (Chs. II, XI, XIX, XX).

5. "Host" nation support of logistical operations (Chs. IX, X).

6. Supply operations in pursuit warfare and in the retreat (Chs. III, IV, XIII, XIV, XVI, XVIII).

7. Theater relations with the zone of interior and the ports of embarkation on such issues as logistical organization, supply requirements, and manpower (Chs. XII, XVI).

8. Quartermaster preparations for amphibious operations (Chs. II, IX, X, XI).

9. Quartermaster organization in a combat zone (Chs. III, IV, XII, XIII, XIV).

10. Local procurement of goods and services (Chs. II, V, VII, X, XII, XV, XVII).

11. Feeding and clothing prisoners of war (Chs. III, IV, V, VII, XV, XVII).

12. Salvage operations in forward areas (Chs. III, VII, XX).

13. Care of the dead (Chs. III, IV, VIII, XIX).

**THE SIGNAL CORPS: THE EMERGENCY (TO DECEMBER 1941).** By *Dulany Terrett*. (1956, 1986; 383 pages, 37 illustrations, appendix, bibliographical note, glossary, index, CMH Pub 10–16.)

**THE SIGNAL CORPS: THE TEST (DECEMBER 1941 TO JULY 1943).** By *George Raynor Thompson, Dixie R. Harris, Pauline M. Oakes*, and *Dulany Terrett*. (1957, 1978; 621 pages, 44 illustrations, bibliographical note, glossaries, index, CMH Pub 10–17.)

**THE SIGNAL CORPS: THE OUTCOME (MID-1943 THROUGH 1945).** By *George Raynor Thompson* and *Dixie R. Harris*. (1966, 1985, 1991; 720 pages, 4 tables, 77 illustrations, appendix, bibliographical note, glossaries, index, CMH Pub 10–18.)

During World War II the Signal Corps provided, as it had traditionally done, both strategic and tactical communications. As both a combat arm and a technical service, a status it shared only with the Corps of Engineers, it was responsible for the doctrine and equipment used by every Army communicator. Thanks to the technological advances of the 1920s and 1930s, electronic signals carried the voice of command from Washington to the most distant theater of operations. Although FM radio had been developed for tactical use by the eve of World War II, pigeons continued to roost within the Signal Corps' inventory. By 1945, despite instances of heroic service, especially in Italy, their days as Army communicators were numbered. These winged messengers, survivors of a simpler era, could not compete with such electronic battlefield devices as the walkie-talkie. The story of this communications revolution is contained in these three volumes. Advances in electronics, especially radar, were second in importance only to that of nuclear fission as an application of scientific knowledge to the fighting of a technological war. However, in the development of many other electronic devices, such as the proximity fuze, Signal Corps research efforts were also significant.

Of the technical services, the Signal Corps was the least prepared in 1941 for what lay ahead. The War Department's prewar planning grossly underestimated the demands for communication that the kind of war in which the United States was about to engage would impose. *The Emergency* examines this planning. It sketches the growth of the corps from its birth in 1860 to the outbreak of World War II in Europe in 1939 (Chs. I–III). The narrative establishes the breadth of the corps' mission and describes its organization, doctrine, and programs of research and development, since all of these deeply affected its activities in World War II. The emphasis of the volume is nonetheless placed on the events of the period from 1939 to December 1941. Each of the main activities of the corps is treated: research and development; procurement, testing, and evaluation; the storage, distribution, and maintenance of devices and systems of communication; and the elaborate training programs needed to see that all of these activities were accomplished effectively. Subsequent volumes continue the coverage of these areas during the war years.

*The Test* begins when two young Signal Corps soldiers at their radar set on Oahu detected the enemy's bombers winging their way in to attack Pearl Harbor. In the months that followed, the corps was almost overwhelmed by the weight of demands for men, equipment, and globe-circling administrative communications systems. The Signal Corps nevertheless ultimately rose to the challenge, providing communications of unprecedented scope and variety. By mid-1943 the corps had passed its first major test in the deserts of North Africa.

*The Outcome* follows the Signal Corps through the subsequent theaters of combat: from the assault landings in Sicily and Italy; through the hedgerows of France; to the jungles of the CBI and the Southwest Pacific. The second half of the volume is devoted to discussing such major activities as electronic warfare, signal security and intelligence, and photography. The authors carry the Signal Corps' story past V–J Day to the first attempt at space-age signals, Project Diana, early in 1946.

In communications as in other areas, World War II required enormous cooperative effort. Thus, the interaction between the War Department, other military agencies, the Allies, and the civil communications industry loom large in these narratives. Although conflicts between these groups are presented from the stand-point of the Signal Corps, each volume has endeavored to do justice to other points of view in examining and presenting the evidence. The last chapter of the second volume (XVI) examines what was perhaps the most critical of these controversies, the jurisdictional conflict between the Chief Signal Officer and the Commanding General of the Army Service Forces (ASF) over the level of command at which control of Army communications should be exercised. This wartime power struggle was resolved in 1946 with the dissolution of the ASF, and the Chief Signal Officer regained direct control over the Army's communications, but the organizational conflict remained without a solid solution, until the McNamara reforms of the 1960s.

A useful feature of the first and third volumes is the appendix in which most of the Signal Corps' World War II equipment is listed and explained in terms intelligible to a layman. The list in volume III has been modified to reflect the discontinuance of certain items.

Key topics:

1. The conflict between mass production of instruments of war and technological improvements (II, Ch. XV).

2. Industrial capacity and plant expansion in the communications industry (II, Chs. I, VI, XV; III, Ch. XII).

3. Small business contributions and subcontracting (II, Ch. XI).

4. Extent and effect of international aid (lend-lease) programs (II, Chs. I, XV).

5. Materials shortages and conservation and substitution measures (II, Ch. VI; III, Ch. XII).

6. Contract termination and renegotiation (II, Ch. XV; III, Ch. XII).

7. Stock control and storage (II, Ch. XV; III, Ch. XIII).

8. Expansion of storage facilities and development of improved depot procedures (II, Chs. VI, XV; III, Ch. XIII).

9. Effect of the 1942 reorganization of the War Department on the Signal Corps (II, Chs. III, XVI).

10. Prewar radar experimentation in the United States and in foreign countries (I, Chs. I, II, VII).

11. Development of the Army's first radar sets, 1937–40 (I, Chs. II, V).

12. The Tizard Mission (I, Ch. VII).

13. Radar proliferation and specialization (I, Chs. VII, X, and App.; II, Chs. III, IX, X, XII; III, Ch. I).

14. The introduction of FM and crystal control into the U.S. Army's radio communications (I, Chs. VI, VII; II, Ch. VIII).

15. The dawn of space-age communications (III, Ch. XIX).

16. Army photographic responsibilities, organization, and contributions: combat photography, V-Mail, training films, still photography, photographic training (I, Chs. III, IV, IX; II, Ch. XIII; III, Ch. XVII).

17. Development of the wartime aircraft warning system (I, Chs. III, VI, XI; II, Chs. I, II, III, IV, V, VII, X, XIV).

18. Signal training and signal schools (I, Chs. II, VI, VIII; II, Chs. I, II, VII, XI;

III, Ch. XVI).

19. Manpower problems in the Signal Corps, military and civilian (II, Chs. I, II, XI; III, Chs. VII, XI, XVI).

20. Labor supply problems and the Signal Corps labor organization (II, Ch. XV; III, Ch. XII).

21. Signal wire and radio equipment (I, Chs. II, V, VI, IX, and App.; II, Chs. III, VIII; III, Ch. XV).

22. Signal radar equipment: airborne and ground (I, Chs. V, VI, VII, X, XI, and App.; II, Chs. III, IX, XI; III, Chs. XIV, XV, and App.).

23. Development and use of radio link (relay) equipment in the U.S. Army (II, Ch. VIII; III, Chs. III, IV, VIII, IX).

24. Extending administrative and command communication facilities around the world (I, Ch. XI; II, Chs. I, IV, V, X, XIV; III, Chs. II–IX, XVIII).

25. Alaska communications and the Alaska Communications System (I, Ch. I, XI; II, Chs. V, XIV).

26. Pigeon communications (I, Chs. I, III, IX; II, Chs. XII, XIV; III, Chs. II, III).

27. Wartime contracting and procurement organizations and procedures in the Signal Corps (II, Chs. I, VI, XI, XV; III, Ch. XII).

28. Effect of patents and licensing agreements on wartime procurement (II, Ch. XI).

29. Spare parts supply (II, Ch. XI; III, Chs. V, XIII).

30. Inspecting signal supplies: organization, procedures, and problems (II, Chs. VI, XV; III, Ch. XII).

31. Packing and packaging, waterproofing, and tropicalization of signal supplies (II, Ch. XV; III, Chs. VII, XII).

32. Relations with and support of the Army Air Forces (I, Ch. X; II, Chs. III, VIII, IX, X, XVI; III, Chs. VII, XIV, XV, XVIII).

33. Signal intelligence, security, and countermeasures (II, Chs. VII, XIV; III, Chs. X, XI).


**THE TRANSPORTATION CORPS: RESPONSIBILITIES, ORGANIZATION, AND OPERATIONS.** By *Chester Wardlow*. (1951, 1980; 454 pages, 12 tables, 7 charts, 28 illustrations, 4 appendixes, bibliographical note, glossaries, index, CMH Pub 10–19.)

The movement of men and supplies, en masse, over great distances became in World War II one of the most vital military interests of the powers engaged, particularly of the Western Allies. Movement overseas, in particular, presented them with problems whose solution spelled the difference between failure and success in defeating the Axis powers. This and the two succeeding volumes on the Army's Transportation Corps are written with an awareness of the importance of effective transportation in bringing to bear the power of the U.S. Army and in delivering military supplies to the British Commonwealth, the USSR, and China, where and when needed to carry out the strategic plans of the Allies.

The Transportation Corps was created after the United States entered the war to overwatch the Army's interest in these matters and to provide the facilities required to move its men and supplies. As the youngest of the seven "technical services" brought together under the control of General Somervell's Army Service Forces in March 1942, the corps was responsible for obtaining the Army's share in the services of common carriers in the United States (by rail, highway, and inland waterways) and in shipping on the high seas. It also supervised the great system of ports of embarkation; organized and operated the rail and truck transportation the Army developed to supplement these services; and assembled and administered, loaded and unloaded the Army's fleet of troopships, hospital ships, and freighters.

This volume covers antecedents and origins of the corps; the difficulties overcome in constituting this latecomer among the Army's services and rendering it efficient; its internal organization in Washington and in the field; its relations with other elements in the Army Service Forces and the overseas commands of the Army; and the measures adopted to ensure economy and efficiency in the use of ports and ships. Also treated are its cooperation and conflicts with the Navy, the Interstate Commerce Commission, the Office of Defense Transportation, the War Shipping Administration, and the British Ministry of War Transport.

Key topics:

1. Transportation as a factor in strategic planning (Ch. I).

2. The shipping crisis in World War II and the Army's measures to meet it (Chs. V, VI, VIII).

3. Wartime relations of military and civilian agencies (Ch. VI, IX, XI).

4. Adaptation and conversion of peacetime public services to war use (Chs. V, VIII, IX).

5. Relationship of the technical services to the Army Service Forces (Ch. III).

6. The American shipbuilding achievement (Ch. V).

7. The special position given the Army Air Forces in the transportation field (Ch. III).

8. The cost of delayed planning to meet the Army's transportation needs (Chs. II, III).

9. Wartime organization:

   a. Office of the Chief of Transportation (Ch. III).

   b. Field establishments of the Transportation Corps (Ch. IV).

10. Control of port utilization and ship employment (Chs. IV, V, VIII).

11. The operation of the Army's wartime fleet and ports (Chs. VII, VIII).

12. The Transportation Corps and the Navy (Ch. VI).

13. The Army's wartime relationship with the railroads and other inland carriers (Ch. IX).

14. The Army's own carriers and their administration (Ch. X).

**THE TRANSPORTATION CORPS: MOVEMENTS, TRAINING, AND SUPPLY.** By *Chester Wardlow*. (1956, 1978, 1990; 564 pages, 40 tables, 12 charts, 59 illustrations, bibliographical note, glossaries, index, CMH Pub 10–20.)

This volume deals extensively with movement, the heart of the Transportation Corps mission. The narrative focuses on the massive movements of men and materiel within the zone of interior and between the United States and overseas theaters of operations.

In meeting its responsibilities in the zone of interior the corps was drawn into active relationships with the common carriers of the United States by rail, highway, and waterway and with the civilian Director of Defense Transportation, in the effort to ensure proper handling of essential civilian traffic as well as extraordinary military demands, since nonmilitary traffic was also greatly increased by the war. The author also deals with the problems of the Chief of Transportation in providing shipping capacity, the most needed and scarcest logistical requirement of the war, to move troops and supplies to the overseas theaters of operations. This responsibility required collaboration with the U.S. Maritime Commission, the War Shipping Administration, and the British Ministry of War Transportation, under direction of the Joint and Combined Chiefs of Staff. In examining these relationships the author particularizes the role of the Chief of Transportation and his corps in the broader picture presented in the volumes on *Global Logistics and Strategy*.

The work takes up the conflicts of jurisdiction, common to all the technical services, which the Chief of Transportation had with Headquarters, Army Service Forces, over the issue of centralization of function and control. Also treated are disputes with the Army Air Forces, since the exemption of air transport from the control of the Transportation Corps made it more difficult for it to ensure prompt and uninterrupted deliveries and to enforce traffic priorities.

In the training and timely deployment of specialist officers and troops the Chief of Transportation had special difficulties since neither his office nor the corps had been established until three months after Pearl Harbor. The effect of this late start on training and procurement was never fully overcome.

Key topics:

1. Limitations on the supply of transportation equipment and its mobilization for wartime use (Chs. I, III, IV).

2. Collaboration of the Army and the railways in wartime (Chs. I, III, IV, VIII).

3. Operation of ports of embarkation and debarkation (Chs. II, III, V).

4. Control of the flow of military freight traffic in the United States (Chs. IV, V, VIII).

5. Conflict of military and civilian interests (Chs. II, III, IV, VIII).

6. Inter-Allied shipping control (Ch. II).

7. International aid; lend-lease (Ch. III).

8. Security problems in wartime (Chs. I, II, V).

9. Operation of special troop trains (Ch. I).

10. Transportation problems involved in furlough travel (Ch. I).

11. Staging areas and troop staging at ports of embarkation (Chs. II, III, VIII).

12. Troopships and troopship administration (Ch. II).

13. Transportation of ammunition and explosives (Ch. V).

14. Transportation officers, specialists, and troop units; requirements and training (Ch. VI).

15. Transportation equipment for theaters of operations: requirements and procurement (Ch. VII).

16. Movement of military patients (Chs. I, III).

17. Handling of prisoners of war (Ch. I).

18. Movement of soldiers' dependents (Ch. III).

19. Repatriation of war dead (Ch. III).

20. Maintenance and spare parts (Ch. VII).

21. Research and development (Chs. VII, VIII).

22. Mounting of amphibious assault forces (Chs. II, V).

**THE TRANSPORTATION CORPS: OPERATIONS OVERSEAS.** By *Joseph Bykofsky* and *Harold Larson*. (1957, 1972, 1990; 671 pages, 3 tables, 7 charts, 12 maps, 17 illustrations, bibliographical note, glossaries, index, CMH Pub 10–21.)

*Operations Overseas* treats the role of the corps in providing transportation for American forces and equipment overseas on a large scale, over invasion beaches, in ports, and on internal lines of communications by rail, highway, and waterway, since indigenous facilities were in most cases inadequate. Employment of local manpower and facilities was indispensable, and the authors describe the problems of language, labor relations, pilferage, safety, and military security that the corps had to meet under widely diverse conditions around the globe. Given a shortage of trained American transportation personnel, it had often to rely on untrained service and combat troops, while its problems were multiplied by the scarcity of base and storage facilities in the Pacific, North Africa, and the Aleutians; by the widespread destruction of ports and railroads in Europe; and by long and unsatisfactory lines of communications in North Africa and Iran and in the China-Burma-India Theater. Its operations were also hampered by the tendency of overseas commands to use oceangoing vessels as floating warehouses, which, for example, created massive shipping tie-ups off the coast of Normandy and in the Pacific. In Europe the corps had to meet the crisis that arose from inadequate provision of heavy motor transport equipment and drivers in planning for the invasion of the Continent in 1944, a deficiency that had grave effects after the breakout at St. Lo when the rapidly advancing American armies outdistanced their supply.

Key topics:

1. Railways as bulk carriers in support of military operations in North Africa, Sicily, and Italy (Chs. IV, V); in northwestern Europe (Chs. VI, VII, VIII); in the Philippines (Ch. X); in Iran (Ch. IX); in Alaska and western Canada (Ch. II); and in India and Burma (Ch. XII).

2. Use of inland waterways to augment available means of transport (Chs. II, VIII, IX, XII).

3. Inter-Allied planning and coordination of movements in theaters, particularly in connection with the buildup of U.S. forces in Britain (Ch. III); the conduct of operations in the Mediterranean (Chs. IV, V); and the planning and execution of the cross-Channel invasion (Chs. X, XI).

4. Utilization of indigenous manpower and facilities, especially in the United

Kingdom (Ch. III); the Mediterranean (Chs. IV, V); northwestern Europe (Chs. VI, VII, VIII); Iran (Ch. IX); Australia (Ch. X); India and China (Ch. XII).

5. Control of shipping in unified commands (SWPA and POA) dependent primarily on water transportation (Chs. X, XI).

6. Over-the-beach operations of supply in the Aleutians (Ch. II); the Mediterranean (Chs. IV, V); France (Ch. VI); and the Pacific (Chs. X, XI).

7. The role of motor transport in providing flexible support for advancing armies (Chs. II, IV–X, XII).

8. Animal transport in Sicily and Italy (Ch. V).

# Special Studies

# Special Studies

The nine volumes comprising the special studies topics are grouped together here because they do not easily fit into any previously covered subseries. However, the reader will find in them a wealth of information on topics that would have profound effects on a postwar society, from the birth of the American military industrial complex (*Buying Aircraft*) to social issues *(Women's Army Corps* and *The Employment of Negro Troops)* that have continued to play a controversial role in the history of the Republic. Though not envisioned at the time, many of the seeds of change brought on by the Second World War, and which would eventually affect both the future military and civilian societies at large, are covered in considerable detail in these volumes.

**CHRONOLOGY: 1941–1945**. Compiled by *Mary H. Williams*. (1960, 1989; 660 pages, glossaries, index, CMH Pub 11–1.)

This massive compilation establishes the sequence of events in World War II from the time the first bombs fell on Pearl Harbor on 7 December 1941 until the surrender of the Japanese aboard the USS *Missouri* in Tokyo Bay on 2 September 1945. A reference work to the United States Army in World War II, the volume details the tactical events of the war day by day, thus giving the reader a measure of the scope of global coalition warfare so that he can begin to grasp the relationship of the innumerable parts to the whole.

This volume emphasizes the ground actions of the U.S. Army in its various operations in Africa, Europe, the Middle East, Southeast Asia, the Far East, the Pacific, and the Western Hemisphere. Events are related at the appropriate level, including battalion and lesser units as well as regiment, division, corps, army, and army group. In addition, the combat actions of Army, Air, Navy, and Marine Corps units and of British, French, Soviet, and other Allied armed forces, as well as those of the enemy, are given in as much detail as space limitations allow. General events of historical import also appear in their proper places.

The value of this well-indexed book is twofold. In one volume the general reader and the student of military history have a ready reference to the whole war during that period in which the United States participated and can quickly check individual facts and dates. In addition, they are able to observe at a glance the progress of the combat operations on a global level for any given day or follow the progress of a single unit day by day to the conclusion of a specific campaign.

**BUYING AIRCRAFT: MATERIEL PROCUREMENT FOR THE ARMY AIR FORCES.** By *Irving Brinton Holley, jr.* (1964, 1989; 643 pages, 23 tables, 9 charts, 36 illustrations, 3 appendixes, bibliographical note, glossary, index, CMH Pub 11–2.)

In the last chapter of *Buying Aircraft,* I. B. Holley, jr., concludes that the process of procuring aircraft for the U.S. Army Air Forces during World War II was as much a weapon of war as the fighters, bombers, and guns procured. The author's specialized study of aircraft procurement bridges the gap between the larger volumes on industrial mobilization and wartime production, such as *The Army and Economic Mobilization* and *The Army and Industrial Manpower,* and the various volumes in The Technical Services subseries that focus on the detailed research, development, and procurement of military materiel for the specific combat and service components of the War Department.

The long years of modest aircraft procurements for the Army Air Service and Air Corps between the wars adversely affected the growth of the American airframe, engine, and components manufacturing industry and discouraged the development of assembly line production methods. The Air Corps Act of 1926 further exaggerated problems by mandating a set of restrictive procedures that governed military aircraft procurement in the following years. When President Franklin D. Roosevelt created the first of his large aircraft production targets in November 1938 in response to the deteriorating situation in Europe, existing Air Corps studies of industrial mobilization were inadequate to handle such a large program. Nevertheless, the aircraft production orders that were now expected to flow encouraged aircraft manufacturers to begin much-needed plant expansions, and the outbreak of war in Europe in September 1939 accelerated that trend as foreign orders and Roosevelt's emerging foreign and national security policies stressed American preparedness. The quick defeat of Poland, the sudden collapse of France, and the ensuing isolation of Great Britain created a sense of national emergency and spurred congressional action that finally removed the procurement restrictions in 1940–41.

The leaders of the Air Corps struggled from 1939 until Pearl Harbor to resolve its key aircraft procurement problems, among them how to define actual requirements for air weapons and spares without an accepted air doctrine and reliable attrition figures for air combat. Moreover, the evolving U.S. economic mobilization and war production structure provided other variables that complicated Air Corps procurement planning and procedures. The final form of aircraft production planning emerged only in late 1942 under the War Production Board (WPB) and its various aircraft production sections and the Joint Aircraft Committee and its subordinate Air Service Unit at Wright Field, Ohio.

Central to the success of wartime aircraft production was the development of new plant capacity through expansion of existing facilities and the building of entirely new aircraft plants. After much discussion between the government and aircraft industry, most new capacity was completed during 1941–43 under the auspices of the Defense Plant Corporation which built government-owned production and assembly facilities for operation by the aircraft and also automobile manufacturers. The large automobile companies, which specialized in assembly line mass production, approached production problems much differently than the aircraft manufacturers who were accustomed to job shop production relying on highly skilled workers. Production of B–24s at Ford's newly built Willow Run, Michigan, facility tested the automobile industry's approach to aircraft production using special tooling, subassemblies, and semiskilled labor. Modification centers were established to make changes and improvements in production line aircraft so that serial production would not be disrupted.

Successful aircraft procurement depended heavily upon the contracting process and the subsequent administration of the contracts. During the war the Army Air Forces constantly revised its air materiel procurement organization and procedures. Procedures for negotiating and administering various types of contracts changed as experience was gained in thousands of large and small procurements. The author rightly devotes significant coverage to the mundane but critically important aspects of contract negotiation and administration and the hard lessons learned in aircraft procurement and production during the war.

Key topics:

1. The effect of congressionally mandated prewar procurement limitations on the development of an efficient aircraft industry that could provide a ready wartime productive capacity (Chs. II–VII).

2. The importance of prewar mobilization planning for effective industrial mobilization (Chs. II, V–XIII).

3. The problems faced in developing realistic prewar requirements for military aircraft procurement and production (Chs. VII, X, XI).

4. The evolution of Army Air Corps and Air Forces organization for aircraft procurement (Chs. IV–VII, XII, XIX).

5. The role of the government in developing the aircraft plant capacity required to sustain the Allied war effort, such as the role of the Defense Plant Corporation, tax-amortization policies, and private capital expansion (Chs. VI–VII, XI–XIV).

6. The role of the automobile industry in manufacturing aircraft during World War II (Chs. VII, XIV, XX).

7. Development of procedures for contract negotiations, administration, and termination in aircraft procurements (Chs. XV–XVIII).

8. Use of cost-plus-fixed-fee (CPFF), fixed-price, and price adjustment contracts for aircraft procurement (Chs. XV–XVII).

9. Problems of allocation of limited aircraft, airframe, engine, and component production capacity between the Army Air Forces and U.S. Navy and within the War Department (Chs. XIX, XX).

10. The roles of the National Defense Advisory Commission (NDAC), Office of Production Management (OPM), and War Production Board (WPB) in developing the policies and procedures for organizing, developing, and administering the nation's productive capacities in general and the aircraft industry in particular (Chs. IX–XIV, XIX, XX).

11. The importance of President Franklin D. Roosevelt in establishing the national aircraft production goals and programs during the prewar years (Chs. VII–XI).

12. Statistics for wartime aircraft and engine production (Ch. XX).

**CIVIL AFFAIRS: SOLDIERS BECOME GOVERNORS**. By *Harry L. Coles* and *Albert K. Weinberg*. (1964, 1986; 932 pages, map, glossary, 2 indexes, CMH Pub 11–3.)

As a documentary history, this volume illustrates the evolution of civil affairs policy and practice in the Mediterranean and European Theaters of Operations during World War II. It deals with U.S. Army and Anglo-American planning and operations in the sphere of relations with civilians in certain liberated and conquered countries in Europe during the war, prior to the invasion of Germany. Although the Army had not considered civil affairs preparation essential prior to World War II, during the war it created the Civil Affairs Division at the War Department level to coordinate all civil affairs planning and training. For the first time, extensive recruiting and training programs were organized, and G–5 (civil affairs and military government) staff sections were added at the theater army, corps, and division levels.

Not only did soldiers become the administrators of civilian life for the Army's immediate needs, they also became the executors, and sometimes the proposers, of national and international political policy. This broader role was the result of the inability of the Allies to agree on specific political aims until after active hostilities were over, if then. In this policy void, U.S. and British military authorities were often responsible for the gradual transition to a postwar national and international order with only general guidelines from higher authorities.

The materials presented in Part I, concerned with the preparatory and organizational stage, suggest that the President's decision to entrust the civil affairs responsibility to the Army was because civilian authorities were unready to undertake the mission. Documents in Part II show the difficulties of fitting civilian institutions into the context of battle and a military framework, thus indicating additional rationale for leaving military authorities in exclusive control. Part III reveals that, despite this experience, Allied authorities planning for the liberated countries of northwest Europe still proposed to delegate civil affairs to indigenous civilian authorities, insofar as was possible. Operations are dealt with in Part IV, which show that conditions during and immediately following hostilities made it necessary for the Allies to render these authorities substantial assistance in the area of civil affairs. The compilation of documents appear to make it clear that the issue of military-versus-civilian administration was far less important than the issue of military values versus civil-political values, and it was in the latter area that the most serious difficulties arose.

Key topics:

1. Arguments over civilian or military control of civil affairs (Ch. I).

2. Civilian civil affairs activities in French North Africa and gradual military involvement (Ch. II).

3. Creation of a military organization to undertake civil affairs activities (Chs. III–VI).

4. Military government/civil affairs operations in Italy (Chs. VII–XXI).

5. Planning for civil affairs operations in Europe (Chs. XXII–XXIV).

6. Military government/civil affairs operations in western Europe (Chs. XXV–XXXII).

**THE EMPLOYMENT OF NEGRO TROOPS**. By *Ulysses Lee*. (1966, 1986, 1990; 740 pages, 12 tables, 5 maps, 38 illustrations, bibliographical note, glossary, index, CMH Pub 11–4.)

By the time Japan surrendered in 1945, some 700,000 black Americans, almost 10 percent of the total force, were serving in segregated Army units throughout the world. Yet, as this volume makes clear, segregation presented insurmountable impediments to the efficient training and employment of this significant segment of U.S. strength and its debilitating effect on the morale of black troops constantly threatened their usefulness. A war that began with black Americans demanding that their right to fight included complete integration of black servicemen into the armed forces, a prime aim of the nascent American civil rights movement.

*The Employment of Negro Troops* examines in detail the Army's prewar planning for the use of black soldiers that was based on its perceptions of segregated troops in World War I. But its plans for the carefully restricted use of a limited number of black soldiers were radically transformed by the great influx of black draftees produced by the nondiscrimination clause of the Selective Service Act of 1940 and by pressures brought to bear on an administration generally disposed to accommodate the growing power of the black voter. Much of this pressure was focused on the War Department through the efforts of the Special Aide to the Secretary of War on Negro Affairs, Judge William H. Hastie. Appropriately in a volume whose subject transcends the usual considerations of military manpower, Hastie's demands are thoroughly evaluated and contrasted with those of his successors.

The volume also analyzes in detail the recruitment of blacks, many unskilled and undereducated, and the challenge of transforming them into soldiers for an Army that for the most part resisted their presence, questioned their competence, and clearly intended to use almost all of them as unskilled laborers and service troops. It also examines the Army's continuing problem in developing suitable leaders for segregated units. Commanders were most often assigned because of their supposed understanding of blacks (southerners) or because they had failed to make the grade elsewhere. Black officers, on the other hand, were given only limited command responsibility. Prejudice and racial stereotyping tended to destroy their morale and kept many from achieving their leadership potential. By midwar, poor leadership, underutilization, and low morale had combined with the severe discrimination suffered by black soldiers both in the military and civilian community to spark widespread racial violence, what the author calls the "Harvest of Disorder."

The task of bringing the Army more closely into line with its announced policy of separate-but-equal treatment fell to Assistant Secretary of War John J. McCloy, operating through the Advisory Committee on Negro Troop Policies. Working closely with Chief of Staff General George C. Marshall, McCloy and his committee succeeded in winning assignments for black units in the overseas theaters. Eventually two black infantry divisions as well as a number of separate tank, tank destroyer, and artillery battalions and combat support units saw action. At the same time the highly publicized "Tuskegee Airmen," and other black air units were trained and deployed in the war against the Germans. The majority of black soldiers, however, continued to be employed in service units around the world, performing important duties but ones that tended to reinforce old stereotypes about blacks as soldiers.

The integration of black infantry platoons in the divisions along the European battlefront was important as a sign of future change and merits special attention in this volume. Smashing a favorite segregationist argument, the performance of these units was free of any racial problems. Their competence, along with that of thousands of other black soldiers, portended the racial transformation of the Army into a fully integrated force just six years later.

Key topics:

1. Army racial policies, 1920–45 (Chs. I, II).
2. Organization and training of black troops (Chs. V, IX).
3. Racial violence in the Army (Chs. IV, VIII, XII, XV).
4. Black women in the Army (Ch. XIV).
5. The deployment and operations of black air units (Ch. XVI).
6. Physical fitness of minority soldiers (Ch. X).
7. Effect of morale on military performance (Ch. XI).
8. Selective Service and military manpower policy (Ch. XIV).

**MILITARY RELATIONS BETWEEN THE UNITED STATES AND CANADA: 1939–1945**. By *Stanley W. Dziuban*. (1959, 1974, 1990; 432 pages, 7 tables, 1 chart, 1 map, 14 illustrations, 5 appendixes, bibliographical note, glossary, index, CMH Pub 11–5.)

This volume records the military cooperation between the United States and Canada during World War II. Diplomatic discussions and negotiations figure prominently in this record, not only as the prelude and basis for joint military plans and efforts, but also in resolving a wide variety of problems incident to those joint efforts that had a political impact.

Originating when the low ebb of British fortunes in the Battle of Britain confronted both the United States and Canada with what seemed an imminent threat to an unprepared continent, cooperation was at first directed to preparation for a coordinated defensive deployment of forces and materiel. Once the safety of the United Kingdom was assured, collaboration largely took the form of measures to facilitate the use by the United States of the geographical, industrial, and military potential of Canada as part of the North American base supporting Allied efforts on the battlefronts of Europe and the Pacific.

Pushing his study into the postwar period, the author also describes the "roll-up" of the extensive United States deployments, facilities, and supply stockades in Canada. He then describes the revitalization of the wartime military cooperation with the outbreaks of the Cold War by 1947.

Key topics:

1. Conduct of bipartite international military cooperation by means of a politico-military board of two coordinate sections (Ch. II).
2. Command structure requirements, in a framework of bilateral cooperation, to

assure adequate military responsibility and authority (Chs. IV, V, VII, VIII).

3. Factors bearing on the defense of North America in a conventional war (Ch. IV).

4. Development of strategic plans and deployments for joint defense of northern North America (Chs. IV, V).

5. Difficulties attending the development of military bases in arctic North America (Chs. VI, VII, VIII).

6. Problems—political, legal, economic, and psychological—incident to large-scale deployments on friendly foreign soil remote from the combat zone (Chs. VII, VIII, XI).

7. Psychological problems of a big nation–small nation partnership in joint defense (Chs. III, VIII, XI).

8. Organization, equipment, training, and employment of an integrated binational force (the First Special Service Force) (Ch. IX).

9. Problems presented to a host government by the great complexity of U.S. Army and Navy organizational structure in Canada (Ch. V).

10. Funding, constructing, and operating base facilities for joint defense (Chs. VIII, XI, XII).

11. Friendly foreign forces and questions of civil and criminal jurisdiction (Ch. XI).

12. Control of air traffic and of military bases by friendly foreign forces (Ch. XI).

13. Disposition of logistical facilities constructed by friendly forces on foreign territory (Ch. XII).

14. Coordination of war production and economic mobilization (Ch. III).

15. The Destroyer-Base Agreement of 1940:

a. Its relation to the initiation of U.S.-Canadian military collaboration (Ch. I).

b. The impact of the agreement and U.S.-Canadian military collaboration on the relationship of Newfoundland to the Dominion of Canada (Chs. I, V, VII).

**REARMING THE FRENCH**. By *Marcel Vigneras*. (1957, 1986, 1989; 444 pages, 5 tables, 6 charts, 1 map, 45 illustrations, bibliographical note, glossaries, index, CMH Pub 11–6.)

This volume tells how the French ground, naval, and air forces available for use against the Axis from mid-1941 to the end of World War II were rearmed, trained, and committed to combat. The narrative focuses on the part played by the United States, especially by the War Department and the U.S. Army, since the commitment, while shared with the British, was largely American, and the rearmed units generally fought as part of larger American commands.

The undertaking was only one of many such American assistance efforts and not the greatest in terms of the volume of equipment involved. More American resources, for example, went to the USSR, the United Kingdom, and China (see *Global Logistics and Strategy* for these). But in the case of the French the forces receiving aid were emerging outside their national home base and therefore lacked the logistical support normally provided by a zone of interior. In this and in other respects the French effort was thus a unique experience.

The volume's "Prologue" provides a brief review, with pertinent statistics, of the assistance similarly extended by France to an unprepared America in 1917–18. But the dramatis personae of the World War II story are the American President, the British Prime Minister, and their civilian advisers; the Joint and Combined Chiefs of Staff, the War Department General Staff, the Army Service Forces, and the agencies charged with direct responsibility for rearming and training the French; and finally the officials of the French High Command and French governmental authorities.

The controversy over the timing and extent of rearmament, in which the American, British, and French authorities were involved long before the Allied landings in North Africa and for months afterward, is one of the major themes of the book. The author deals with the establishment and implementation of the successive rearmament programs concurrently with the evolution of the decisions that made them possible. The programs aimed at rehabilitation of the forces raised in North Africa (Prologue, Chs. I–III, V–VII, IX) and in metropolitan France (Chs. XVIII–XXI), and included the air force (Chs. XII, XXII), the navy (Chs. XIII, XXII), and Sovereignty and Territorial forces (Chs. VII, IX). The part played by the United States in the Anglo-American effort to support the Resistance forces is also described (Ch. XVIII).

*Rearming the French* also describes in detail the organization, role, and activities of the various agencies involved in French rearmament and training: the Joint Rearmament Committee (Ch. XVII), the Joint Air Commission (Ch. XVII), the Rearmament Division of SHAEF (Ch. XXIII), and the French Training Section (Chs. XVII, XXIII). Also discussed are two major problems that were a source of continuing concern for the Allied high command: the difficulties encountered by the French in establishing a sound supply system of their own and the resultant persistent shortage of French service troops (Chs. VII–X, XX). Another was the training of the rearmed units (Chs. XIV, XXIII).

Key topics:

1. French political developments affecting the course of rearmament operations, in particular the tug of war between Giraud and de Gaulle (Chs. V, VI, IX) and the Stuttgart and north Italy incidents (Ch. XXI).

2. The part played by rearmed French units in combat operations (Ch. XI).

3. The abortive French attempt to organize and equip forces for the liberation of Indochina (Ch. XXIV).

4. The effect of Franco-American political relations (Ch. IX).

5. The language barrier (Ch. XIV).

6. Differences in national customs, food habits, and clothing sizes (Ch. XVI).

7. Requirements for liaison, armament, and training personnel (Ch. XIV).

8. Procedures for assignment and delivery of equipment (Chs. I, XX). (For a treatment at greater length, see both volumes of *Global Logistics and Strategy.)*

9. Surplus stocks and equipment shortages (Chs. VIII, X).

10. Control over rearmed units (Ch. IX).

11. Special supplies and miscellaneous equipment (Ch. XVI).

**THREE BATTLES: ARNAVILLE, ALTUZZO, AND SCHMIDT**. By *Charles B. MacDonald* and *Sidney T. Mathews*. (1952, 1989, 1991; 443 pages, 44 maps, 44 illustrations, order of battle, bibliographical note, glossaries, index, CMH Pub 11–7.)

The three engagements presented in this book are described in detail to illustrate the nature of battle in Europe during World War II at the small-unit level. They supplement the campaign histories of the European and Mediterranean Theaters of Operations where the amount of small-unit material that can be included in a history is limited by the large size of the forces that have to be followed. In these three studies a microscope is applied, so to speak, to actions which either have been or will be related, minus the detail of these presentations, in the campaign histories of those theaters.

The three battles here described were selected not for their importance but for two other reasons. One was the availability of information, including contemporary interviews, which would permit the author to maintain the small-unit level through an entire operation or to a natural conclusion. The other was a desire for actions in which the role of arms and services other than infantry could be presented in a variety of tactical situations. Each study therefore provides an opportunity to examine the interplay of small parts on an actual battlefield.

The first of the three, "River Crossing at Arnaville," is an account of two attempts to establish bridgeheads across the Moselle River near Metz, France, in September 1944: one a failure, the other a success. Two infantry regiments of the 5th Division and a combat command of the 7th Armored Division were the major units engaged. "Break-Through at Monte Altuzzo" describes a successful but arduous attempt by elements of a regiment of the 85th Infantry Division to penetrate the Giogo Pass in the Appenines, also in September 1944. "Objective: Schmidt" is primarily the story of the 112th Infantry of the 28th Division in an unsuccessful operation against the village of Schmidt within the Huertgen Forest in Germany in 1944.

The narrative in each case goes down from regiments, battalions, and companies to platoons, squads, and individuals. The story of higher headquarters and of high-level communications and decisions is related only as necessary for an understanding of the operations of these lower units. Attention is focused on the problems and achievements of soldiers and officers of small units on the battlefield.

The tactical framework of the three studies is varied: a river crossing, mountain warfare, and forest and village fighting. Accounts are included of most of the normal offensive and defensive assignments to be expected of infantry units under these tactical conditions. Detail is sufficient in text and maps for study of all three actions as case histories with little or no recourse to additional material.

In addition to the overall accounts, fairly complete instructional examples may be obtained on a number of subjects, including the following:

1. Inadequate intelligence (Arnaville, Ch. I; Altuzzo, Chs. I, II; Schmidt, Ch. III).
2. Poor command coordination (Arnaville, Ch. I; Altuzzo, Ch. II).
3. Smoking operations to conceal bridge-building activity (Arnaville, Ch. III).
4. Employment of artillery against fixed defensive works (Arnaville, Ch. I).
5. Engineers in role of infantry (Schmidt, Chs. IV–VII).

6. Engineer bridging operations (Arnaville, Ch. III).

7. Communications failures (Altuzzo, Ch. II).

8. Erroneous messages and situation reports (Altuzzo, Chs. I–III; Schmidt, Chs. V–VI).

9. Organization of a deliberate defensive position (German) (Altuzzo, Ch. I).

10. Supply problems (Arnaville, Ch. I; Altuzzo and Schmidt, passim).

11. Methods of counterattack (German) (Arnaville, Ch. I; Altuzzo, Chs. II, V; Schmidt, Chs. III–VI).

12. Inadequate security (Schmidt, Chs. II–VI).

13. Tanks and tank destroyers in close support (Arnaville, Chs. III, IV; Schmidt, Chs. III–VI).

14. Panic (Arnaville, Ch. II; Altuzzo, Chs. II, III; Schmidt, Chs. III, V, VI).

Other general subject areas found throughout the work include: morale, misdirected artillery fire, attempts by tactical air to isolate a local battlefield, close support artillery, reluctance of the individual to fire, combat fatigue, loss of direction, patrolling, medical evacuation, propaganda leaflets, personnel replacements, equipment shortages, tank-infantry coordination, tanks in an antitank role, and employment of armor under adverse conditions of weather and terrain.

**THE WOMEN'S ARMY CORPS**. By *Mattie E. Treadwell*. (1954, 1985, 1991; 841 pages, 13 tables, 2 charts, 97 illustrations, 5 appendixes, bibliographical note, glossary, index, CMH Pub 11–8.)

This comprehensive and detailed record of the wartime Women's Army Corps (WAC) is the first full-dress official history prepared about a corps of women in the military service of any nation. Although the work is pitched at the policy and planning level, rather than at the hundreds of individual units that made up the WAC, the author has managed to include many samplings of the ordinary female soldier's routine duties and reactions—enough to give the reader a real sense of what life was like for a woman in the Army and what it was like for the Army to have women in it.

The spotlight is often focused on WAC headquarters and on its wartime head, Col. Oveta Culp Hobby. Her efforts to make the WAC a going and useful concern were sometimes handicapped by the confusion that existed in the field and on occasion even in Washington about the extent of her authority and responsibilities as Director, WAC. Nevertheless, the chronological account of the establishment and conduct of the Women's Army Corps is considerably amplified by a topical discussion of various aspects of the Army's problems in employing womanpower.

The WAC at its peak strength of 100,000 constituted an enviably large group for study. Because of its around-the-clock control of personnel, the Army had access to information not easily obtainable by business or industry. Its discoveries in general appear valid and reliable, not only for militarized groups, but for most nonmilitary institutions or businesses which train or employ women. The observations on health, fatigue, accident rates, and psychological patterns, as well as the discoveries in the fields of training, housing, clothing, feeding, and disciplining groups of women, offer valuable insights, including heretofore unpublished statistics, in the social history of the Army.

Part One, "The Organization and Growth of a Women's Corps," covers the origin (Ch. I) and establishment (Ch. II) of the Women's Army Auxiliary Corps, the struggles of the first year (Chs. III–XI), the conversion and integration into the Army (Chs. XII, XIV), attempts to revive recruiting (Ch. XIII), and the removal of the Director's Office to the G–1 (personnel) Division (Ch. XV). Part Two, "World-Wide Employment," begins with the account of the employment of women in the Army's three major commands: the Army Air Forces (Ch. XVI), the Army Ground Forces (Ch. XVII), and the Army Service Forces (Ch. XVIII). The next chapter (Ch. XIX) describes their employment in the Medical Department's Auxiliary Service Force (ASF). The succeeding three chapters describe the WACs in overseas theaters: the Mediterranean theater, including North Africa (Ch. XX); the European theater (Ch. XXI); the Southwest Pacific Area (Ch. XXII); and other overseas theaters (Ch. XXIII). The Office of the Director, WAC, is discussed in the last chapter (XXIV).

Part Three, "War Department Policy Concerning the Women's Army Corps," deals with legal, social, and moral problems (Ch. XXV); housing, food, and clothing (Ch. XXVI); the employment of personnel: enlisted women (Ch. XXVII), officers (Ch. XXVIII), overseas shipment (Ch. XXIX), and minority groups (Ch. XXX); health and medical care (Ch. XXXI); training (Ch. XXXII); the leadership of women (Ch. XXXIII); and recruiting and publicity (Ch. XXXIV).

Part Four, "Last Days of the Wartime WAC," describes the WACs in the closing months of the war (Ch. XXXV) and in the throes of demobilization (Ch. XXXVI). The title of the final chapter is self-explanatory: "Evaluation and Recommendations."

Women's services, other than the WAC, discussed in this volume are the following:

1. Air Wacs (see Index: also under "Army Air Forces").
2. Army Nurse Corps (see Index).
3. British women's services (see Index: "Auxiliary Territorial Services," and App. B).
4. Canadian women's services (see Index).
5. Women's service in the U.S. Coast Guard (see Index: "SPARS").
6. WASP (see Index: "Women Air Service Pilots," and App. D).
7. WAVES (see Index: "Women Accepted for Volunteer Emergency Service").
8. WIRES (see Index: "Women in Radio and Electrical Service").
9. Women's Reserve, Marine Corps (see Index).
10. WOWs (see Index: "Women Ordnance Workers").

**MANHATTAN: THE ARMY AND THE ATOMIC BOMB**. By *Vincent C. Jones*. (1985, 1988; 660 pages, 7 maps, 3 tables, 5 charts, 93 illustrations, appendix, bibliographical note, glossaries, index, CMH Pub 11–10.)

This volume describes the U.S. Army's key role in the formation and administration of the Manhattan Project, the World War II organization which produced the atomic bomb that contributed significantly to ending the conflict with Japan and marked the beginning of the postwar atomic era. It relates how the Army, starting in 1939, became increasingly involved in the research activities initiated by American and refugee scientists into the military potentialities of atomic energy, spurred on by the conviction that the Axis powers already had under way programs for the development of atomic weapons. With the United States entry into the war after the attack on Pearl Harbor (1941) as an active participant, America's wartime leaders took immediate measures to expand the research and industrial efforts required to develop atomic weapons. To administer this enlarged program, they turned to the Army as the organization best suited to cope with its special security, priority, manpower, and other problems in an economy geared to all-out war production.

The Army took over the atomic bomb program in the early summer of 1942. By that time much of the basic scientific research and development prerequisite to building the plants and testing the methods for weapon design and production had been completed. To form and oversee an atomic bomb construction and production organization, the Army turned to its own Corps of Engineers, with a long and distinguished history of supervising large-scale building projects. The corps responded to its newly assigned task by adopting organizational procedures used on all its major construction projects. It set up a new engineer "district" under the command of a district engineer, who temporarily established his headquarters in the facilities of the corps' division engineer in New York City. For reasons of security the new district's project was designated the Laboratory for Development of Substitute Materials (DSM), but unofficially became known as the Manhattan District because of its New York location.

This history of the Manhattan Project takes a broadly chronological approach but with topical treatment of detailed developments. The focus of the narrative is from the vantage point of the Manhattan Project organization, as it functioned under the direction of Maj. Gen. Leslie R. Groves and such key scientific administrators as Vannevar Bush, James B. Conant, Arthur Compton, and J. Robert Oppenheimer, responding to policies originating at the top levels of the wartime leadership. The volume begins with a prologue designed to provide the reader with a brief survey of the history of atomic energy, explaining in layman's terms certain technical aspects of atomic science.

The remainder of the book takes the reader through the turnover of the project administration to the Army and the beginnings of the atomic age. Discussion of technological problems and issues are presented in nontechnical prose. This volume ends where it began with the project being transferred back to civilian control.

Key topics:

1. The history and theoretical basis of atomic science before the outbreak of World War II (Prologue).

2. The contributions during World War II of civilian scientific agencies, such as the National Defense Research Committee (NDRC) and the Office of Scientific Research and Development (OSRD), to the program for design and manufacture of an atomic bomb (Ch. I).

3. How the Army successfully organized and administered several projects that

enabled American industry to build and operate massive production facilities essential to the making of atomic bombs (Chs. III, IV, Part II).

4. The technical problems involved in the production of fissionable materials (uranium and plutonium) for use in atomic weapons (Part II).

5. The difficulties and complexities of interchanging scientific information and personnel among Allies in wartime as exhibited in the collaboration between the United States and Great Britain on atomic matters in World War II (Ch. X).

6. The special problems of designing and managing a project-wide security system based upon the principle of compartmentalization of information (Ch. XI).

7. The planning, building, and administering of new communities for civilian war workers and military personnel serving at atomic installations in Oak Ridge, Tennessee; Richland-Hanford, Washington; and Los Alamos, New Mexico (Chs. XXI–XXIII).

8. The essential elements for interservice collaboration as exhibited by the leaders of the Manhattan Project and the Army Air Forces in the strategical and tactical planning and the on-site preparations for the atomic bombing of Hiroshima and Nagasaki, Japan, in August (Ch. XXVI).

# Pictorial Record

# Pictorial Record

In the narrative volumes of the United States Army in World War II series, it is possible to include only a limited number of the thousands of pictures taken by photographers of the U.S. armed forces. The Pictorial Record, a subseries of three volumes, has therefore been compiled to show in greater detail the conditions under which the combat forces lived, the methods by which they were trained, the weapons they and their opponents used, the terrain over which they fought, and the support they received from the technical branches of the U.S. Army, the U.S. Army Air Forces, and the U.S. Navy.

Two volumes of the subseries deal with the war against the European Axis and the third covers the war in the Pacific and in the China-Burma-India Theater. Each volume is arranged in sections that follow the course of the war chronologically; the written text has been kept to a minimum, each section having a brief introduction recounting the major events covered therein. The three volumes together give a comprehensive pictorial survey of the U.S. Army's operations in Africa, Europe, the Middle East, Southeast Asia, the Far East, and the Pacific.

**THE WAR AGAINST GERMANY AND ITALY: MEDITERRANEAN AND ADJACENT AREAS.** (1951, 1988; 465 pages, 5 maps, 495 illustrations, glossary, index, CMH Pub 12–2.)

This volume deals with operations in North Africa, the Middle East, Sicily, Corsica, Sardinia, the Italian mainland, and southern France.

**THE WAR AGAINST GERMANY: EUROPE AND ADJACENT AREAS.** (1951, 1989; 448 pages, 7 maps, 568 illustrations, glossary, index, CMH Pub 12–3.)

Covered in this volume are the buildup in the United Kingdom, the air offensive in Europe, and the Normandy, Northern France, Rhineland, Ardennes-Alsace, and Central Europe Campaigns.

**THE WAR AGAINST JAPAN.** (1952, 1988; 471 pages, 13 maps, 566 illustrations, glossary, index, CMH Pub 12–1.)

Here are depicted training in Hawaii, Australia, and New Caledonia; defeat in the Philippines; the campaigns in the Solomons, New Guinea, New Britain, the Admiralties, the Aleutians, the Gilberts, the Marshalls, and the Marianas; the return to the Philippines, Iwo Jima, and Okinawa; and the operation of the supply line to China through Burma and India.

# World War II Sources

The volumes produced in the United States Army in World War II series represent one of the most ambitious historical writing projects ever conducted. Popularly known as the "Green Books," the series itself constitutes but a fraction of the historical material available on World War II. A broad foundation of records and recollections, carefully documented and annotated in the footnotes of each volume, supports the entire series, but even the vast amount of documents referenced cover only the activities of the U.S. Army in rather broad terms. For any detailed study of a particular aspect of the Army in World War II a researcher has more than 17,000 tons of Army records produced during the war years with which to contend, as well as a huge volume of prewar records which provide essential background to events taking place during the war.

Beyond Army records there are Navy, Air Force, and Marine Corps records which document their participation in the war, as well as those of other government agencies. Obviously a historian can eliminate large segments of official records simply based on the topic of inquiry. If the focus is strategy, then only the records of the highest levels will be of interest; if, however, the focus is on particular military operations, then the records of the participating units will be the primary sources of information. Additional primary documentation can be found in personal diaries and memoirs of the leading participants in the war, which often go beyond the official records in presenting details of how and why decisions on the conduct of the war were made. Whether one has been a student of the war for some time or is simply interested in a specific aspect of the war, the following information is thus no more than a limited introduction to the wealth of source material available.

## RECORDS SUPPORTING THE UNITED STATES ARMY IN WORLD WAR II

The records and documents collected and used by the historians who researched and wrote the individual volumes in the series are located in a variety of collections. Each of the volumes has a brief bibliographic note which outlines the sources used in the preparation of that volume and where they may be found. After each volume was written and published the notes, working drafts, and documents retained by the author(s) were gathered together and retired to the National Archives and Records Administration (NARA) in Washington, D.C. Sources noted in a volume as being at the U.S. Army Center of Military History (CMH) in Washington, D.C., have generally been transferred to the collections at NARA.

Unpublished historical manuscripts prepared by Headquarters, War Department agencies; Army Service Forces; Technical Services; Army Ground Forces; and

Army commands located in the continental United States and in the theaters of operations are on file at CMH. Microfilm copies of these documents are also on file in the library of the U.S. Army Command and General Staff College at Fort Leavenworth, Kansas.

Documents with the War Department decimal prefaced by Misc., HRC, or GEOG are part of the Historical Records Collection at CMH. Transcripts of interviews conducted by the author(s) while researching are located both at the U.S. Army Military History Institute (MHI) at Carlisle Barracks, Pennsylvania, and in the Military Reference Branch, Textual Reference Division, of NARA. Diaries cited in the volumes may be in a variety of places. Some are at MHI, others at CMH, and still others were returned to private owners.

Official records created by Headquarters, War Department agencies; the Supreme Headquarters, American Expeditionary Forces; the Army Service Forces; and the Army Ground Forces will be found in the Military Reference Branch, Textual Reference Division, of NARA. Official records created by Army commands within the continental United States and the Army Technical Services and World War II operational reports are in the Suitland Reference Branch, Textual Reference Division, of NARA.

Official photographs and posters from all the services including the Army are on file in the Still Picture Branch, Special Archives Division, of NARA. Official Army motion picture films and sound records are in the Motion Picture, Sound, and Video Branch, Special Archives Division, of NARA. NARA also has reproduced some of the motion pictures in video tape format and maintains special collections of many of the commercial motion pictures which deal with World War II.

Army maps, charts, blueprints, aerial photographs, posters, and architectural drawings of fortifications, U.S. government buildings in and around Washington, D.C., and some buildings on Army installations are filed with the Cartographic Architectural Branch, Special Archives Division, of NARA in Washington, D.C.

Official personnel records for all members of the Army are at the National Personnel Records Center in St. Louis, Missouri. Unfortunately, about 85 percent of the records were destroyed in a fire at the center in 1973. Alternative sources of information on individuals who served in the Army in World War II include the General Accounting Office pay vouchers filed in the National Personnel Records Center; Selective Service records in the Regional Archives Division of the Federal Records Centers; the courts-marshal records from the Clerk of the Court, Army Judiciary, in Falls Church, Virginia; the Veterans Administration in Washington, D.C.; and in the records of state adjutants general and county and municipal governments.

Personal papers and related material of senior leaders not found in the institutions may be found at MHI. In addition special collections, such as the Eisenhower or MacArthur libraries, contain extensive archives on the participation of the more notable American leaders in World War II.

There are also large collections of unit histories, of widely varying lengths, at MHI, CMH, and other military libraries. CMH also holds a number of collections of historical material prepared or gathered by CMH historians in the course of preparing the Green Books.

## OFFICIAL HISTORIES

The Green Books of the United States Army in World War II constitute the official history of the U.S. Army. The series was published by the Government Printing Office, and individual volumes are still available from that agency. While the other services do not have anything directly comparable to the Green Books, each has produced or sponsored a service history which covers World War II.

The Navy's semiofficial history of the war was written under an arrangement with Samuel Eliot Morison, at the time professor of history at Harvard University. His *History of Naval Operations in World War II*, published by Boston's Little, Brown and Company in fifteen volumes, is based primarily on official records. The activities of the Air Force are covered in *The Army Air Forces in World War II*, edited by Wesley Frank Craven and James Lea Cate. The multivolume series was originally published by the University of Chicago Press and is now available through the Government Printing Office. A five-volume *History of U.S. Marine Corps Operations in World War II* has also been published by the Government Printing Office.

A number of other Allied participants in World War II have also produced multivolume official histories of their own that are widely available in the United States. The British *History of the Second World War* series was edited by J. R. M. Butler and published by Her Majesty's Stationery Office. Australian participation in the war is covered in *Australia in the War of 1939–1945*; the *Official History of the Canadian Army* was published by the Queen's Printer and Controller of Stationary; and Bisheshwar Prarad edited the *Official History of the Indian Armed Forces in the Second World War 1939–45,* which was prepared under the auspices of the Combined Inter-Services Historical Section (India and Pakistan). The *Official History of New Zealand in the Second World War 1939–1945* was published by the Government Printer of New Zealand. Multivolume official histories of the war are either under way or have been published in France (Service Historique de l'Armee); the Federal Republic of Germany (Militaergeschichtliches Forschungsamt); and in the former Soviet Union, although its historians have not yet been able to produce an agreed-upon version.

## FOREIGN RECORDS

Official German war records held by the United States after World War II have been returned to Germany, but microfilm copies are still held at NARA and are available to researchers. NARA also holds over two thousand manuscripts written by German authors under the auspices of the U.S. Army. These are cataloged and indexed in the *Guide to Foreign Military Studies 1945–54,* a collection maintained by the Military Reference Branch, Textual Reference Division, of NARA.

Information on German operations in World War II is also available in a series of monographs prepared by CMH German-language qualified historians. These authors based their studies on official German records captured or seized during the war and on the postwar manuscripts cited above. These manuscripts are available at CMH and MHI.

French records available on microfilm from NARA's Military Reference Branch include a nearly complete collection of daily journals, situation reports, and operations orders for all French divisions, corps, and higher headquarters. These documents are supplemented with large numbers of French Army plans, reports, special studies, and other records and information provided by the Service Historique de l'Armee.

The Japanese record of World War II is not as complete as the German, but there are still considerable sources of material. One series of monographs was prepared after the war by former Japanese Army and Navy officers under the supervision of the Historical Section of the Far East Command in Tokyo. These studies, covering a wide variety of war-related topics, are available at CMH. The Far East Command also assembled a collection of *Imperial General Headquarters* directives and orders for the wartime period. NARA also holds a microfilm collection of records of the Japanese Army and Navy Ministries dating from the turn of the century which were seized by U.S. authorities after the war. The original records have been returned to the government of Japan. The largest number of foreign military records are, of course, to be found in the country of origin.

## JOURNALS AND SECONDARY SOURCES

Many articles have appeared in military professional journals both during and after World War II which cover a wide variety of topics. Prominent among the American periodicals are the *United States Naval Institute Proceedings, Army* (and its predecessors, *Combat Forces Journal* and the *Infantry Journal*), *Military Review*, and *Marine Corps Gazette*; these are supplemented by such publications as the British *Journal of the Royal Service Institute* and the French *Revue Historique de la Deuxieme Guerre Mondiale*. Unfortunately these periodicals are not usually indexed in the *Reader's Guide to Periodical Literature*, although some use can be made of the *National Defense Review* issued from 1947 to 1955 by the Army Library at the Pentagon and the *Air University Periodical Index* of the Air University Library, Maxwell Air Force Base, Alabama.

Almost all public, academic, and military libraries have large sections of secondary works devoted to the history of the Second World War. The most comprehensive guides to these works are *World War II: Books in English, 1945–65*, compiled by Janet Ziegler and published in 1971 by the Hoover Institution Press in Stanford, California, and a supplement published by the American Committee on the History of the Second World War in pamphlet form entitled *A Select Bibliography of Books on the Second World War in English Published in the United States, 1966–1975*. Yet interest in World War II remains intense, and the continued outpouring of articles, books, dissertations, and even memoirs on the conflict makes the creation of even semidefinitive bibliographical guides exceedingly difficult.

# Index

USAPPC - 2-04357 - 320-735 - 11/92